Sails for Profit

A Complete Guide to Selling and Booking Cruise Travel

Jeanne Semer-Purzycki
Robert H. Purzycki

Prentice Hall
Upper Saddle River, New Jersey 07458

Library of Congress Cataloging-in-Publication Data
Semer-Purzycki, Jeanne.
    Sails for profit : a complete guide to selling and booking cruise
travel / Jeanne Semer-Purzycki, Robert H. Purzycki.
        p.   cm.
    ISBN 0-13-958117-0
    1. Cruise lines—Handbooks, manuals, etc.   2. Cruise lines—Study
and teaching.   3. Tourist trade—Marketing.   4. Ocean travel—Study
and teaching.   5. Ocean travel—Handbooks, manuals, etc.
I. Purzycki, Robert H.   II. Title.
G550.S46 1999
338.4'791—dc21   99-6058
                                                                              CIP

Acquisitions Editor: Neil Marquardt
Editorial Assistant: Jean Auman
Editorial Production Services: Tally Morgan, WordCrafters Editorial Services, Inc.
Cover Art Director: Jayne Conte
Cover Designer: Tom Nery
Prepress Manufacturing Buyer: Ed O'Dougherty
Managing Editor: Mary Carnis
Director of Production and Manufacturing: Bruce Johnson
Marketing Manager: Frank Mortimer, Jr.

©1999 by Prentice-Hall, Inc.
Simon & Schuster/A Viacom Company
Upper Saddle River, NJ 07458

ISBN 0-13-958117-0

Prentice-Hall International (UK) Limited, *London*
Prentice-Hall of Australia Pty. Limited, *Sydney*
Prentice-Hall Canada, Inc., *Toronto*
Prentice-Hall Hispanoamericana, S.A., *Mexico*
Prentice-Hall of India Private Limited, *New Delhi*
Prentice-Hall of Japan, Inc., *Tokyo*
Simon & Schuster Asia Pte. Ltd., *Singapore*
Editora Prentice-Hall do Brasil, Ltda., *Rio de Janeiro*

Contents

4 Itineraries, 69

5 Resources and References, 101

6 Sales Techniques, 157

7 Booking and Documentation, 179

Glossary, 191

Preface

The cruise industry is a gold mine that is virtually untapped! It's a gold mine because the cruise experience ranks the highest in customer satisfaction. According to a recent travel industry survey, more than 90 percent of people who have sailed on a cruise vacation came back totally satisfied with the experience; they would consider taking another cruise in the future. The potential for repeat cruise customers is very high in comparison with other types of vacation products.

This gold mine is untapped because only *10 percent* of vacation travelers have taken a cruise; this leaves more than *90 percent of vacation travelers* as potential cruise customers.

Even with only 10 percent of the market share, the cruise industry generates the *second largest source of revenue for U.S. travel agencies* after airline ticket sales. According to a survey conducted by *Travel Weekly* (Figure P.1),

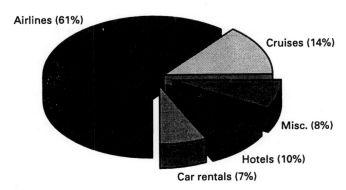

Airlines (61%)
Cruises (14%)
Misc. (8%)
Hotels (10%)
Car rentals (7%)

Figure P.1

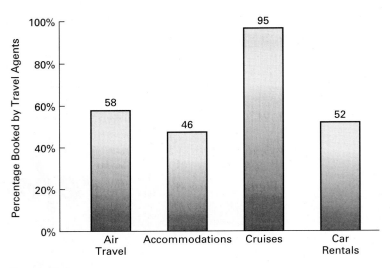

Figure P.2

cruise sales account for approximately 14 percent of total travel agency revenue; this translates into more than $14.5 billion (airlines account for 61 percent of total agency revenue, with $61.2 billion).

Another interesting statistic shows that the majority of cruises are booked through travel agencies and not by passengers directly through the cruise lines. Figure P.2 shows the percentage of each of four leisure products—air travel, accommodations, cruises, and car rentals—that is booked through travel agencies. Compared to all other products, the majority of cruises—approximately 95 percent—are booked through travel professionals. Because of the wide variety of different types of cruises, itineraries, and prices, people need to rely on professionals for guidance and recommendations when selecting cruises.

Who takes cruises? The answer may surprise you. Many people think that cruise vacations are only for the very old and the very rich. Nothing can be further from the truth! The demographics or standard profiles of cruise clients and what they buy are shown in the box opposite in terms of age, gross annual household income, cruise length selected, and average cruise cost.

More than one-third of all cruise clients are under age 34; the majority of them, approximately 62 percent, are under age 54. Approximately half of all cruise clients have a gross annual household income of under $28,000; the average cruise cost per day is between $200 and $250 per passenger, per day. The majority of cruise vacations taken—61 percent—are one week in length.

DEMOGRAPHICS OF CRUISE CLIENTS

Age		Gross Household Income	
18–34	37%	Under $15,000	20%
35–54	25%	$15,000–$28,000	28%
55+	38%	$28,000+	52%

Cruise Length		Cruise Cost		
1–5 days	23%	Low	$100	per day
6–8 days	61%	High	$800+	per day
9–17 days	15%	Average	$200–$250	per day
18+ days	1%			

So, take a vacation product that is the second leading revenue generator for travel agencies, coupled with a vast untapped market, and you have a very important vacation product that plays a major role in the huge travel and tourism industry. This book will familiarize you with all of the important aspects of selling cruise vacations, from basic nautical terminology to shipboard life, world itineraries, and key resources that can help you market and sell cruises effectively to future clients.

Before starting this course material you must do one thing: get rid of any personal bias or prejudice you may have about cruises, especially if you have not taken one yourself! This is rule number one in any type of sales encounter; what you may or may not like personally should have nothing to do with counseling your clients in an objective and open-minded manner. You are suggesting what is best for your clients. Let's face it—the saying "Different strokes for different folks" certainly applies in any selling situation.

HOW THIS BOOK IS ORGANIZED

This book is intended for anyone who is studying to become a travel sales professional or someone who is already working in the travel industry. The text is divided into seven chapters.

Introduction

Chapter 1 presents a brief history of cruise travel that brings today's cruise industry into perspective and affords a glimpse into the future of this important travel sector. It also introduces some basic nautical terminology—important words and phrases used in industry resources that you should also use in conversations with your future clients and industry peers.

What It's Like to Take a Cruise

Chapters 2, 3, and 4 show you what it's like on board a cruise ship. Before you can sell cruises, you have to know what you are selling! You will learn the "Who's Who" of today's ships—popular cruise lines, the ships they operate, where they go, and what markets they target. Also, these chapters show what it's like to take a cruise—from dining and entertainment to shopping, gambling, and sightseeing. Chapter 4 shows you where today's ships travel—all over the globe: everything from a mysterious river cruise through the jungles of the Amazon to a trip through the frozen reaches at the bottom of the world on an Antarctic ice-breaker! You will be convinced that there is a cruise experience for just about every traveler.

Your Resources

Chapter 5 provides examples of the standard resource books and guides that you will use when selling cruise travel. This includes the cruise brochure, which is both an important sales tool and an informational resource. It's a sales tool because it presents the "sizzle": colorful and dramatic pictures of the ship and its passengers, and scrumptious descriptions of dining, dancing, entertainment, and much more. It's an informational resource because it presents the "steak": the terms and conditions of booking and buying a cruise, which must be clearly understood by both the travel counselor and the client.

Sales Techniques and Booking

Chapters 6 and 7 are probably two of the most important chapters of all. You can know your product inside and out, and know where to go for help, but if you don't close the sale, nothing happens! That's the bottom line: your objective is to sell something! As a travel professional, you serve as a matchmaker; you need to know who your client is, be able to make good recommendations, overcome objections, and finally make the booking. Chapter 7 deals with what comes after the sale: the mechanics of booking a cruise and the standard paperwork involved in this type of transaction.

FEATURES OF THIS TEXTBOOK

This is an interactive textbook. Learning is constantly reinforced through frequent student exercises, learning tips, and key terms, which are spread liberally throughout the textbook. These features include:

- *Chapter objectives* that tell you what you need to know or be able to do at the end of each chapter.
- *Key terms* listed at the beginning of each chapter that are defined in the text material.
- A *glossary* of all important terms and abbreviations at the end of the text for easy reference.
- *Checkpoint exercises* presented at frequent intervals throughout each chapter, to help reinforce your understanding of individual concepts.
- *Chapter reviews* that include short-answer, multiple-choice, fill-in, and matching exercises that ensure understanding of stated objectives.

INSTRUCTOR'S MANUAL

The *Instructor's Manual* contains all that is needed to ensure productive and informative class sessions with minimal preparation time:

- A presentation outline.
- A suggested timetable for both full-semester or partial-semester course coverage.
- Teaching tips and discussion topics.
- An answer key to all Checkpoint and Chapter Review exercises.
- A test bank for a written examination.
- Printed masters of key diagrams, forms, and maps to be used as overhead transparencies or printed handouts.

About the Authors

Jeanne Semer-Purzycki is one of the leading authors in travel and tourism education today. In addition to this text, she has written three other textbooks that are being used in hundreds of colleges and proprietary schools throughout the country: *A Practical Guide to Fares and Ticketing*, *A Practical Guide to SABRE Reservations and Ticketing*, and *International Travel, Fares and Ticketing*. She is currently working on an introductory text on the travel industry that will incorporate the latest in computer technology, including the Internet.

During her professional life, Ms. Semer-Purzycki has served as a classroom instructor, curriculum developer, and program and school director on both the college and proprietary school levels. She has also helped to develop training materials on behalf of the Institute of Certified Travel Agents (ICTA) on a contractual basis.

Ms. Semer-Purzycki is currently serving as an education specialist and consultant to colleges and proprietary schools through the Higher Education Assistance Group in Newton, Massachusetts. She earned her master of science degree in education from Central Connecticut College. Her undergraduate work was completed at the University of Vermont, where she earned her bachelor of science degree in education.

This textbook is a culmination of this author's personal travel experience. Ms. Semer-Purzycki has taken more than 24 cruises on itineraries spanning the globe. In addition, she has toured and inspected more than 20 additional cruise ships.

Author Jeanne Semer-Purzycki relaxing during a shore excursion on the Isle of Capri, Italy.

Author Robert Purzycki on deck sailing through the Lynn Canal in Alaska.

Robert H. Purzycki has served as a school director and a classroom instructor in travel education. He is currently teaching travel industry courses at the Travel Education Center, Cambridge, Massachusetts. During his successful career as a travel educator, Mr. Purzycki has been instrumental in designing and implementing travel industry and geography curriculum on both college and proprietary school levels.

Mr. Purzycki earned his bachelor of arts degree in geography from the University of South Florida, and a certificate in Spanish studies from the University of Madrid, Spain. In addition, he has earned his Destination Specialist designation from the Institute of Certified Travel Agents (ICTA) in the areas of the Caribbean, Europe, and the Pacific Rim. He is currently involved with ICTA on an ongoing project-oriented basis.

This author has traveled around the world several times, visiting more than 100 countries. He has cruised on 30 ships and has inspected and toured 35 additional vessels during his travel industry career. Most of the photos for this text were taken by him on his many cruise adventures.

Looking Back and Some Nautical Talk 1

After completing Chapter 1, students will be able to:

- Discuss the important milestones that have occurred from the days of transatlantic passenger service up to today's system of cruise travel.

- Define and identify on a deck plan each of five directional terms:

port	aft
forward	amidships
starboard	

- Define each of the sixteen terms that describe parts of the ship:

berth	ladder
boat deck	main deck
bow	porthole
bridge	stem
bulkhead	stern
center of gravity	superstructure
galley	weather deck
hull	

KEY TERMS

aft	hull
amidships	ladder
berth	main deck
boat deck	port
bow	porthole
bridge	starboard
bulkhead	stem
center of gravity	stern
forward	superstructure
galley	weather deck

A GLIMPSE INTO THE PAST

How long have cruise vacations been around? Did people go on cruises 100 years ago? Two hundred or more? Believe it or not, cruises have been around for thousands of years, since the Romans crossed the Mediterranean Sea by ship to view the ancient pyramids in Egypt!

1819	*Savannah*: Advent of steam travel on transatlantic liners
1840	Samuel Cunard begins transatlantic passenger service
1858	*Great Eastern*: Largest passenger ship built as a steam and sailing vessel, nearly 700 feet long with five smokestacks and six sailing masts.
1897	*Kaiser Wilhelm der Grosse*: Most modern and luxurious steamship of the day
1907	Two passenger liners, the *Lusitania* and the *Mauretania*: First use of steam turbine engines, which heralded the great age of transatlantic luxury crossing
1927	Luxury liner *Ile de France*: First supership and the largest and fastest ship to date
1931	*Normandie*: Most elegant transatlantic liner of the era
1940	*Queen Elizabeth*: Largest transatlantic liner of all time
1948	*Caronia*: First ocean liner built for cruising
1960	More people cross the Atlantic by air than by ship for the first time
1965	*Oceanic*: First ship to be launched as a cruise ship. At 1,600 maximum berths, she is the largest for cruising
1966	Norwegian Caribbean Cruise Line begins service with the futuristic *Sunward* to the Bahamas, the true beginning of modern-day cruises
1988	*Sovereign of the Seas*: Largest cruise ship ever built—2,600 passengers at 73,200 tons, one-week cruises in Caribbean
1996	*Destiny*: At 101,000 tons the largest passenger cruise ship that breaks the 100,000 ton barrier
1999	Royal Caribbean International launches a 130,000-ton cruise ship—the largest ship by the end of the 20th century

Figure 1.1 **Important dates in cruise history.**

Early Sailing Ships

Sea voyages have not always been luxurious and carefree. In ancient times, sea travel was dangerous; people didn't look forward to it. Before 1800, most ships were powered by wind-driven sails. But with the advent of the steam engine in the early 1800s, sea travel became safer, faster, and more comfortable.

In 1819, the *Savannah* became the first steam-powered ship to cross the Atlantic, marking the first time that steam power was used to assist sail power. In 1840, Samuel Cunard, a Nova Scotia merchant, launched the *Britannia*, which was the fastest ship to travel between England and the United States. The Britannia was also the first ship operated by a new company called Cunard Steamship Ltd. The Cunard company is still operating today, which makes it one of the longest operating passenger shipline companies in the world.

As early as 1858, the largest ship that was built up to that time rivaled many of our contemporary ships in length. The *Great Eastern* was the largest passenger ship built as a steam and sailing vessel; it boasted five smokestacks and six sailing masts and approached 700 feet in length. The ship, however, was a financial disaster, being too big for its time in terms of power, its inability to dock, and the expense of operating and maintaining it. It finally ended up as a floating museum and was broken up for scrap in 1889.

Around this time, the majority of ship passengers were European immigrants traveling to the United States. Many of them were immigrating to escape political unrest in their home countries, others because of the economic opportunities that America promised. More than 17 million immigrants made this voyage by passenger liner during the late 19th and early 20th centuries.

The Race for Supremacy

The year 1897 marked the beginning of a race to build the biggest, fastest, and most elegant passenger vessels. The race for supremacy of the high seas was on with such national competitors as England, France, Germany, and the United States. The starting gun of this race resounded when the ship *Kaiser Wilhelm der Grosse* was built by Germany and became the most modern and luxurious passenger ship of its time.

Great Britain joined the race in 1907 with two ships, the *Lusitania*, and the *Mauretania*, both of which used steam turbine engines, heralding a new age of transatlantic speed and luxury crossing. Other ships followed, some with names we all recall: the doomed *Titanic*, which sank on its maiden voyage after hitting an iceberg; the *Olympic*, sister ship to the *Titanic*; and the *Aquitania*. All of these ships were built by the British.

World Wars I and II

With the advent of World War I, passenger ships were stripped of their luxuries and configured to carry troops and supplies. Practically all transatlantic passenger traffic ceased for the duration of the war, from 1914 to 1918. After World War I, the United States curtailed foreign immigration dramatically, and the transatlantic steamers had to find new passengers. As a result of this, the modern-day concept of cruising was born.

In 1927, the luxury liner *Ile de France* was launched, making it the largest and fastest ship to date. It had a very interesting and long career as a passenger luxury liner before World War II, and continued as a troopship throughout the war. It was converted back into a passenger luxury liner after the war and operated as such until its last voyage in 1959.

The *Normandie* was probably the most elegant transatlantic liner of the 20th century. It was built in 1931 with no expense spared. It gleamed with polished wood and brass, was adorned with the most elaborate and beautiful chandeliers, and rivaled any famous museum with its many treasures on view. Sadly, in 1942 the *Normandie* caught fire while it was being converted to a troop ship and sank at the dock to the bottom of New York harbor.

The 1930s heralded not only the most luxurious but also the biggest transatlantic ships. A notable one was the Cunard Line's *Queen Mary*, built in 1936. The *Queen Mary* became the largest and fastest passenger ship up until World War II. The ship was retired in the late 1960s and is now a permanently docked floating hotel, museum, and conference center in Long Beach, California.

The other Queen of the high seas is the original *Queen Elizabeth*, launched by Cunard Line at the beginning of World War II. The early history of this ship was as a camouflaged war ship—carrying troops and supplies rather than passengers. After World War II, it began transatlantic passenger service and continued until it was destroyed by fire in Hong Kong harbor in 1972. At 86,000 tons, it held the distinction for some time of being the world's largest passenger vessel ever built.

Crossings versus Cruises

Up until 1948, all passenger vessels were designed primarily for transatlantic crossings. These early liners were also based on a strict class system. Some of these ships had two classes—first and tourist—while others offered three—first, second, and third. The price you paid for your ticket determined where you were allowed to sleep, dine, and walk on deck, and the types of passenger facilities and services available.

On these earlier ships, the class barriers were vertical; they were much like the first-class, business-class, and coach sections on airplanes. First class on a ship included all passenger decks extending from the front of the ship to the middle; second class ranged from the middle to about three-quarters toward the back; and third class was located at the extreme back end of the ship.

A cruise was different from a transatlantic crossing. A crossing was made to get passengers from point A to point B as quickly and comfortably as possible. A cruise is not only a form of transportation but a way to see new ports of call and do some sightseeing along the way. On a ship designed for cruising, a lot more space must be allocated for dining, entertainment, and other passenger amenities. Also, the earlier ships did not have airconditioning, so they could not be used to sail extensively through warm waters.

Modern Cruising

The first ship actually designed to operate cruises was the *Caronia*, built in 1948. The ship was nicknamed "the Green Goddess" (it was painted three shades of green) and offered lengthy cruises around the world. Other ships soon followed by offering short and long cruises to different ports of call around the world.

The biggest turning point that sounded the death knell to the large transatlantic liners was the advent of the jet age. People were now able to cross the Atlantic in seven hours rather than seven days, and at a fraction of the cost. In 1958, for the first time more people crossed the Atlantic by air than by ship.

Cruising as we know it today was born in 1965, when Home Lines launched the *Oceanic*. This ship was the first one built for the mass market, it sailed round-trip from New York to the Bahamas on weekly cruises.

Cunard Line, realizing that transatlantic service was diminishing and that the short-cruise concept was increasing in popularity, decided to build a ship that could do both: serve as a transatlantic luxury liner during part of the year, and as a cruise ship to warmer destinations such as the Caribbean during the rest of the year. The ship that served as both was the *Queen Elizabeth II*, which still remains today as the only ship offering scheduled transatlantic service during the summer and short cruises and world cruises during the rest of the year.

In 1966, Norwegian Caribbean Cruise Line (the name has been changed to Norwegian Cruise Line, or NCL) was formed as the first company that offered cruises exclusively. All other ship companies up until that time were in the business of transporting passengers; NCCL was the first ship company to offer only cruise vessels. NCCL began service with the futuristic *Sunward*, which sailed three- and four-day cruises to the Bahamas; this was another milestone in the development of cruise vacations as we know them today.

Throughout the 1960s and 1970s, cruise travel flourished. New cruise line companies such as Royal Caribbean Cruise Line (in 1997, the company changed its name to Royal Caribbean International) and Carnival Cruise Line were formed and operated regularly scheduled cruises to places such as the Caribbean and Mexico. These cruise ships were truly a classless society—they offered just one class of service. All passengers, whether they paid the least expensive or the most expensive cruise fare, shared all passenger facilities and services.

Up until the 1980s, cruise ships were relatively small due to market demand. On the average, ships were 15,000 to 30,000 gross registered tons and carried anywhere from 500 to 1,200 passengers.

An important benchmark in cruise travel occurred in 1988, when RCCL introduced the first *megaship*, called *Sovereign of the Seas*. This was the first ship of what was later to be called the *Sovereign-class* of ships. Nothing like it had been built since the *Queen Mary* and the *Queen Elizabeth* of the 1930s. The ship was enormous—it had more than 73,000 gross registered tons and carried 2,600 passengers on one-week cruises through the Caribbean. Royal Caribbean International went on to build several more ships in the same class. Other cruise lines soon followed suit with their own megaliners.

In 1996, Carnival Cruises introduced the *Destiny*, which was the largest passenger ship built to date at 101,000 gross registered tons—taller than the Statue of Liberty and as long as three football fields. In 1998, Princess Cruises introduced the *Grand Princess*, approximately 105,000 tons. This record will soon be broken. Royal Caribbean International is committed to building two ships at 135,000 gross registered tons each to be delivered around the year 2000.

As you can see, the sayings, "Less is more" and "Good things come in small packages" don't apply to cruise travel today.

SAILING INTO THE 21ST CENTURY

The three words that describe what the future holds for the cruise industry are *big, bigger,* and *biggest*! There will also be many more ships to choose from. Cruise lines are betting that they can grab a big share of the 90 percent of travelers who have never cruised before.

All of the major lines, such as Carnival Cruise Line, Celebrity Cruises, Royal Caribbean International, and Princess Cruises, have each ordered several more ships to be built over the next decade. They are all in the megaship range—over 70,000 tons (the average tonnage up until a few years ago was about 30,000) and carrying more than 2,400 passengers. One of the biggest of all is a vessel being built by Royal Caribben International that is slated to begin sailing in the year 2000. It will weigh more than 130,000 tons and carry 3,100 passengers. That's the trend: bigger and more of everything.

The cruise companies know that offering the biggest of everything isn't necessarily going to win them a large share of the untapped cruise market. Ships need to offer the high level of entertainment and recreation that today's consumers now expect. They expect space-age entertainment and effects; traditional magic shows, singers, and stand-up comedians don't cut it anymore, unless there is a lot of glitz, pizazz, lasers, and other pyrotechnics happening on stage at the same time! And that is what the newer and future cruise ships will offer.

Modern ships will offer sophisticated interactive and entertainment systems. From their in-cabin TV screens, passengers can order room service, make spa appointments, browse in "virtual" boutiques, play casino-type games, and select pay-per-view movies. With a swipe of a charge card, passengers can place phone calls to any place in the world right from their cabins. There is even talk about building a ship of approximately 200,000 gross registered tons! It would be designed as a stationary vessel, permanently anchored as its own island in the Caribbean. Passengers would travel to it, by either ferry or helicopter, and the vessel would actually be an entire destination at sea with its own sand beaches, amusements, and recreational facilities. Will it work? Only time will tell!

Checkpoint 1.1 _____

1. What part did the ship *Savannah* play in nautical history?_____

   _____

2. Name one of the oldest passenger shipline companies in the world.

   _____

3. Name the ship built in 1948 that was the first vessel designed to operate cruises._____

4. The majority of passengers on the early transatlantic crossings in the late 19th and early 20th century were _____.

5. Name the two largest transatlantic liners ever built? _____

   _____

6. What event in the mid-20th century doomed many of the large transatlantic liners? _____

7. How does the *Queen Elizabeth II* differ from its predecessors?

   _____

8. Name the first cruise company to offer passenger cruises exclusively in the 1960s. _____

9. Why was Royal Caribbean International's *Sovereign of the Seas* considered a benchmark in cruising when it went into service in 1988?

   _____

10. What is the trend of cruise ships into the 21st century?

_____

_____

Nautical talk

When you visit a foreign country, it's nice to be able to speak the language of that country. If you don't, the next best thing is to know a few key words and phrases in order to make yourself understood. This also applies when you sell cruises to clients and even when you are on a cruise as a passenger. It sounds so much more professional to tell your clients that their cabin is located *starboard amidships* rather than on the right side of the ship toward the middle. Or that the dining room is located in the *stern* rather than in the back end of the ship.

This section includes some key terms that describe directions, types of decks, and parts of a cruise ship—know them by heart! Additional terms are defined in the Glossary.

Deck and Location Terms

Cruise ships have *decks*, not floors. There are passenger decks and decks where only the ship's crew members are allowed. All passenger decks are located above the waterline. Smaller vessels may only have a few passenger decks; large ships or megaships carrying more than 1,800 passengers have up to fourteen passenger decks. The lowest decks on a cruise ship consist of accommodations for the ship's crew, storage areas, and the engine room. Passengers are not allowed to visit these lower decks unless they are on a ship tour.

Each passenger deck is identified by name or letter; deck names differ ship to ship.

For example, on Royal Caribbean International's, *Monarch of the Seas*, the upper passenger decks are named the Compass Deck, the Sun Deck, the Mariner Deck, and the Showtime Deck. The lower passenger decks are usually identified by letters or numbers.

Figure 1.2 is a diagram of a typical cruise ship. It identifies different parts of the ship and their location.

Directional Terms

Figure 1.3 shows a horizontal cross-section of a typical cruise ship; you are positioned above a deck looking down. The front of the ship is pointing toward the right of page 9.

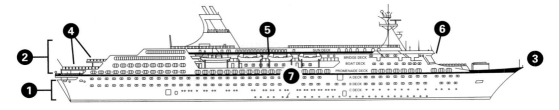

1. **Hull**—The part of the ship that rests in the water; the frame or body of the ship, exclusive of the superstructure.
2. **Superstructure**—The part of the ship above the hull.
3. **Main deck**—The longest deck on the ship; separates the hull and the superstructure.
4. **Weather deck**—Any deck open to the outside.
5. **Boat deck**—The deck where the lifeboats are located.
6. **Bridge**—Navigational and command center of the ship; closed to passengers except upon invitation.
7. **Center of gravity**—The fulcrum or balancing point in the ship; located at the point where a vertical and horizontal line are each drawn through the middle of the ship.

Figure 1.2 **A typical cruise ship.**

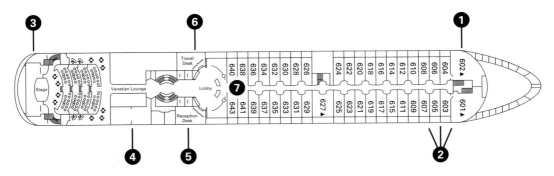

1. **Bow**—The front part of the ship. Example: *"Cabin 602 is located in the bow."*
2. **Forward**—Toward or near the bow or front of the ship. Example: *"The passenger cabins are located forward of the lobby."*
3. **Stern**—The back end of the ship. Example: *"The stage is located in the stern."*
4. **Aft**—Toward or near the stern or back of the ship. Example: *"The Venetian Lounge is located aft of the lobby."*
5. **Starboard**—The right side of the ship facing forward. Example: *"The Reception Desk is located on the starboard side on the Ocean Deck."*
6. **Port**—The left side of the ship facing forward. Example: *"The Travel Desk is located on the portside on the Ocean Deck."*
7. **Amidships** (or **midships**)—In or toward the middle of the ship. Example: *"The lobby is located amidships on the Ocean Deck."*

Figure 1.3 **Horizontal cross-section of a typical ship.**

Additional Terms

Here are some other useful terms you should know. Many of them will be covered in more detail later in the text.

Beam   The width of the ship (amidships) at its widest point.

Berth   (1) A bed in ship's cabin. (2) The location at the pier where the ship docks.

Bulkhead   An upright partition or wall dividing the ship into cabins and compartments.

Companionway or **stair tower**   An interior stairway on a ship.

Course   The direction in which the ship is headed, usually expressed in compass degrees.

Debark or **disembark**   To get off or exit the ship.

Deck   Any floor on a ship, inside or out.

Deck plan   A blueprint or floor plan of a ship's design.

Dock   A berth, pier, or quay.

Embark   To get on board a ship.

Fathom   A measurement of distance (usually depth) in the water equal to six feet.

Free port   A port or place free of customs duty and most customs regulations.

Funnel   A smokestack or "chimney" of the ship.

Galley   The ship's kitchen.

Gangway   The opening through the ship's side and the corresponding ramp by which passengers embark or disembark.

Gross registered ton (GRT)   A measurement of 100 cubic feet of enclosed revenue space within a ship.

Hold   Interior space below the main deck for storage or cargo and where passengers are not allowed.

Knot   A unit of speed equal to one nautical mile per hour (6,080.2 feet), as compared to a land mile of 5,280 feet.

Ladder   Any stairway on the outside areas of the ship.

Leeward   Away from the wind.

Manifest   A list or invoice of a ship's passengers, crew, and cargo.

Pitch   The front-to-back (bow-to-stern) motion of a ship.

Port   The left side of the ship when facing toward the front or bow.

Porthole   Round window or opening on the side of the ship.

Quay   (pronounced *key*) A berth, dock, or pier.

Registry   The country whose laws the ship and its owners are obliged to obey, in addition to complying with the laws of the countries where the ship calls and/or embarks passengers.

Roll The side-to-side motion of the ship.

Stabilizers Finlike, gyroscopically operated devices that extend from both sides of the ship below the waterline to provide more stable motion. This device acts like a wing on an airplane.

Stack A funnel from which the ship's combustion gases are freed to the atmosphere.

Stem The extreme forward point on the ship.

Tender A smaller vessel, sometimes one of the ship's lifeboats, that is used to transport passengers between the ship and shore when the ship is at anchor.

Upper and lower Berth arrangements in a cabin that are similar to bunk beds.

Weather side The side of the ship that is exposed to the wind or the weather.

Windward Toward the wind.

CHAPTER REVIEW

1. Discuss when and why transatlantic steamship travel diminished in popularity. _____

   _____

2. What are two major differences between a transatlantic vessel and a cruise ship of today? _____

   _____

3. Name the first ship built in the 1960s that heralded modern-day cruising.

   _____

4. Discuss the importance of the *Sovereign of the Seas* (operated by Royal Caribbean International) in terms of the evolution of modern-day cruise ships. _____

   _____

5. Match each term with the correct definition on the right.

   a. boat deck   _____ The longest deck on the ship

   b. bridge   _____ Lifeboats are located here

   c. superstructure   _____ Any deck open to the outside

   d. weather deck   _____ The control center of the ship

   e. main deck   _____ The fulcrum (the smoothest ride is here)

   f. center of gravity _____ The upper section of ship

6. An overhead diagram or blueprint of a ship's design that shows all cabins and public areas is called a _____ _____.

7. The middle section of the ship, front to back, is called _____.

8. The side-to-side motion of a ship is called _____.

9. A bed on a cruise ship, or the location at the pier where the ship is moored, is called a _____.

10. The front-to-back motion of a ship is called _____.

11. A bed arrangement in a cabin similar to bunk beds is called _____.

12. Decks on a ship are identified by name, letter, or _____.

13. The _____ is the opening in the ship's hull and the corresponding walkway by which passengers enter or leave the ship.

14. The kitchen on a ship is called the _____.

15. Any wall or partition on a ship is called a _____.

16. Any floor on a ship is called a _____.

17. Any stairway located in the interior of the ship is called a _____.

18. The area used for storage or cargo, where passengers are not allowed, is called the _____.

19. A deck plan of a ship is shown in Figure 1.4. It shows cabin numbers and other passenger areas. Describe the location of the cabins and facilities listed by filling in the blanks. Choose the terms from the following list:

aft   amidships   bow   forward   port   starboard   stern

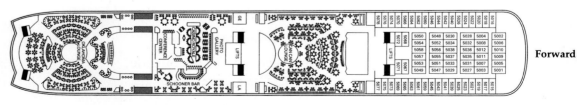

Figure 1.4

a. Cabin 5010 is located _____ or in the _____ section.

b. The Oklahoma Lounge is located _____ or in the

_____.

c. The Photo Gallery is located _____ of the Can Can Lounge.

d. The Schooner Bar is located on the _____ side of the ship.

e. The Can Can Lounge is located in the middle of the ship or

_____.

f. Cabins 5078 and 5076 are located on the _____ side of the ship.

g. You just rode the elevator (or lift) and are now facing the back of the Can Can Lounge. You want to find the Conference Center located on this deck. Would you walk forward or aft? _____

20. Match each nautical term with the correct definition on the right.

a. knot   _____ A dock or pier

b. gross registered   _____ The part of the ship that lies
   ton   above the main deck

c. registry   _____ A device that provides a smoother
                               ride
d. stabilizer
                        _____ A small vessel that carries passen-
e. superstructure   gers between ship and shore

f. weather side   _____ The country under whose laws the
                               ship operates
g. beam
                        _____ The direction away from the wind
h. tender
                        _____ 100 cubic feet of interior space
i. leeward
                        _____ The smokestack or "chimney" of a
j. quay   ship

k. funnel   _____ The side of the ship exposed to the
                               wind or weather

                        _____ A unit of speed equal to one nautical
                               mile per hour

                        _____ The width of a ship at its widest
                               point

Who's Who 2

After completing Chapter 2, students will be able to:

- Name and describe the four general categories of cruise vessels.

- Describe the general characteristics of seven typical passenger-type categories.

- Name major cruise line companies that offer each of the following types of cruise experiences:

  traditional cruises
  tall-masted schooners/windjammers
  river and canal cruises
  expedition/adventure cruises

- Explain how the GRT and standard passenger capacity affect the spaciousness on board a cruise ship.

- Calculate the space ratio when given the GRT and standard passenger capacity.

KEY TERMS

demographics
expedition/adventure cruise
gross registered tons
river cruise
space ratio
standard passenger capacity
traditional cruise
windjammer

INTRODUCTION

There are many different kinds of cruise experiences; from the conventional cruise ship that is like a floating resort to a much smaller, intimate, and slow-moving passenger barge meandering through Europe's inland waterways. Cruise ships cater to every income level and interest. Some appeal to the mass market—people representing a wide spectrum of tastes, styles, interests, and income levels. Others target a specific type of traveler, in a *niche market*.

Ships come in all sizes and shapes. Many of today's newly built ships are so big that they are called *megaships* and accommodate more than 2,000 passengers. Others are small and yachtlike in appearance; they hold no more than a few dozen. Some cruises last only a day or two, while others last for months as they sail around the world.

Ships go just about everywhere in the world. Some cruise ships visit traditional ports in the Caribbean, Mexico, and Alaska; others venture into more exotic waters such as the South Pacific and even Antarctica. Some vacations are even marketed as "cruises to nowhere"; the ship stays at sea during the entire cruise. For these vacations, the attractions are dining, dancing, gambling, and entertainment while on board the ship.

Each ship is designed differently. Some ships resemble floating cities with multi-tiered shopping malls, pools, and health spas; some even have a small-golf course on the top deck! Others are tall-masted schooners where passengers can help sail the vessel or small, intimate luxury barges that offer gourmet food and the best wines!

With all these choices, how do you match the client with the best cruise? To make a successful match, you need to know as much as you can about your clients: Who's traveling—a single person, a couple, a family? What are their ages? What is their budget? Where do they want to go? What do they want to do? Have they cruised before? What are their past travel experiences? Next, you need to know as much as you can about the different cruise ships: What are they like? Where do they go? What do they offer? How much do they cost?

In this section we will first take a look at *who's cruising*—the types of people who go on cruises. Then we will study *what's sailing*—a sampling of the different types of cruise experiences and categories from which to choose.

WHO'S CRUISING?

The best way to put this all in perspective is to find out what type of traveler is attracted to what type of cruise. To be a matchmaker, you not only have to identify different categories of cruise ships, but you also have to categorize people. You can do this through *demographics*—the statistical study of populations with reference to such things as age, budgets, marital status, special interests, and hobbies, for example.

One word of caution: It is difficult to categorize people, their likes, and their dislikes, let alone all of the different types of cruise ships available to sell. A particular cruise ship can satisfy passengers fitting many demographic profiles. Also, people can't be neatly pigeonholed; we all have contradictory tastes and interests. It is not unusual for the same person to enjoy both contemporary rock music and classical music, or to find bungee jumping and attending the opera equally satisfying!

Who's cruising? Cruise passengers are people from all walks of life: lawyers, software programmers, doctors, and corporate executives, along with engineers, actors, farmers, and college students. And they are all traveling either as singles, as couples, or as families.

Where does each one fit? To simplify matters, you can divide all potential cruise passengers into four general demographic groups: *budget*, *mass market*, *upscale*, and *luxury*. Each category is briefly described here with an average cost per day, per person, along with a sample of cruise line companies that target that particular market.

It should be noted here that money is not the only criterion when selecting a cruise. Some clients would spend many thousands of dollars to go on a once-in-a-lifetime cruise to Antarctica, but would never dream of spending the same amount of money for a traditional cruise through the Caribbean.

Budget Market

These ships cater to those who want to take a cruise but at the same price they would pay on a discounted land-based hotel package. Usually, these people are first-time cruisers looking to spend one week or less on their vacation.

Average cruise cost per day, per person: $100–$150

Cruise line examples: Premier Cruise Line, Windjammer Barefoot Cruises

Mass Market

These are the traditional ships that cater to a broad range of passenger types: couples, singles, families, and seniors looking for a typical cruise vacation. In general, these travelers work and have the traditional two weeks' vacation per year. They have saved up for a vacation and are looking for value for their money. They are somewhere within the middle-class income level.

Average cruise cost per day, per person: $200–$250

Cruise line examples: Carnival Cruise Lines, Costa Cruise Lines, Royal Caribbean International, Norwegian Cruise Line (NCL)

Upscale Market

These ships target those who travel frequently and have sophisticated tastes and judgment of what to expect. Money is not a primary concern as long as they receive good value for the money spent. These travelers are generally in the upper-middle-class income level. Many are looking for longer or more unusual itineraries.

Average cruise cost per day, per person: $300–500.

Cruise line examples: Princess Cruises, Holland America Line, Celebrity Cruises, Cunard (*Queen Elizabeth II*).

Luxury Market

These ships cater to travelers who want the very best and for whom price is no object. They expect excellent service, gourmet food, the very best wine selections, and individual pampering.

Average cruise cost per day, per person: $500+

Cruise line examples: Radisson Seven Seas Cruises, Crystal Cruises, Silversea Cruises, Seabourn Cruise Line, Windstar Cruises, Cunard *Sea Goddess*.

*W*HAT'S SAILING?

Now that we have defined who is taking cruises, let's take a look at the different types of cruise experiences. Like people, ships themselves are difficult to categorize! To simplify things, we can break them down into four general categories of cruises: *traditional cruises, masted sailing ships/windjammers, river and canal cruises*, and *expedition/adventure cruises*. Each is described here, along with illustrations and examples.

The Traditional Cruise

This is the most popular and prevalent type of cruise experience. The majority of ships belong in this category. The traditional cruise ship is viewed as an all-inclusive floating resort. It provides everything that the traveler wants, in an all-in-one vacation package: accommodations, transportation, dining, entertainment, sports, and recreation.

Standard cruises are seven to twelve days in length with either seasonal or year-round programs, depending on the destination. The atmosphere or ambience will differ from ship to ship: some ships stress fun and games, a lot of passenger activity, and nonstop entertainment. Others offer a more quiet and relaxing mood.

Figure 2.1 Traditional Cruise: The 1,870-Passenger Celebrity Cruises' *Galaxy*.

Most traditional cruise vacations offer *air/sea packages*, which include round-trip airfare from most U.S. home cities, transfers between the airport and the ship, and all features and amenities on board. Most cruises also offer *pre-tour* and *post-tour* packages that enable passengers to extend their vacation either before or after the cruise. Pre-tour and post-tour packages include accommodations at selected hotels, transfers, and some sightseeing at the destination.

Who travels on traditional cruises? A wide range, from budget to luxury clients.

Masted Sailing Ships/Windjammers

This type of cruise is for those who want to recreate what sailing was all about in earlier times—to feel the wind in their faces and the roll of the sea under their feet.

Figure 2.2 Masted Sailing Ship: Windstar Cruises' *Windsong*.

These vessels are tall-masted schooners that appeal to a wide spectrum of people. *Barefoot windjammers* allow passengers to actively participate in sailing the ship if they want to. Others can sit back and relax on larger, high-tech, super-deluxe ships with computerized sails.

River and Canal Cruises

These are small ships and barges that sail the world's inland waterways of rivers and canals. Although many of these vessels are quite small (sometimes carrying only a dozen or so passengers), some can be very luxurious. These cruises appeal to those who want a lot of scenery, since the vessel is never far from land. The itineraries usually do not include frequent stops in major cities, but rather in small towns and villages that are seldom visited on traditional cruises. River and canal cruises emphasize learning about the culture, history, and heritage of the places visited along the way.

A river cruise may be a luxury steamboat traveling up and down the Mississippi River, or a multi-deck contemporary vessel meandering slowly along the Rhine River in Germany, passing romantic castles and medieval towns. It can also be an adventurous trip up the Nile to discover the mysteries of ancient Egypt.

A canal cruise can be on a luxury barge

Figure 2.3 **River Cruise: Delta Queen Steamboat Company's** *Mississippi Queen* **(foreground) and** *Delta Queen.*

that accommodates only ten or twelve people and offers gourmet food and a wide assortment of wines while traveling through the wine-and-chateaux region of France. Another popular itinerary is a historical but leisurely venture up and down the Thames River in England.

These types of cruises have widespread appeal but generally target those who are well-traveled and are looking for a more culturally enriching and educational trip at a leisurely pace.

Expedition/Adventure Cruises

Travelers choose these types of cruises on the basis of ports of call visited rather than the ship itself; these cruises don't usually provide the wide range of passenger amenities and entertainment that traditional cruises offer.

Expedition and adventure cruises visit more out-of-the-way, exotic destinations, such as the continent of Antarctica or the Galápagos Islands, a wildlife refuge located hundreds of miles off the coast of South America.

People who take these types of cruises want to learn about the places visited. These cruises will have on staff a naturalist, a historian, or other experts to provide lectures and lead field trips; the emphasis is on education rather than recreation.

The type of passengers who take adventure or expedition cruises are similar to those attracted to the river and canal itineraries: the "been there, done that" crowd looking for a new and exciting experience.

Figure 2.5 is a quick, at-a-glance reference chart that lists representative cruise lines with the following descriptive categories: cruise category,

Figure 2.4 Expedition/Adventure Cruise: Clipper Cruise Line's *Clipper Adventure.*

Cruise Line	Cruise Category	Price*	Passenger Category	Target: Singles	Target: Families	Target: Seniors	Target: Adventurers
Abercrombie & Kent	River & Canal	$$$$	Upscale				✗
American Hawaii Cruises	Traditional	$$	Mass Market			✗	
Carnival Cruise Lines	Traditional	$–$$	Mass Market	✗	✗		
Celebrity Cruises	Traditional	$$$	Upscale				
Clipper Cruise Line	Adventure & Expedition	$$$	Upscale			✗	✗
Costa Cruise Lines	Traditional	$$–$$$	Mass Market				
Crystal Cruises	Traditional	$$$$	Upscale			✗	
Cunard— *Queen Elizabeth II*	Traditional	$$$$	Upscale			✗	
Cunard— *Royal Viking*	Traditional	$$$$	Upscale			✗	
Cunard— *Sea Goddess*	Traditional	$$$$$	Luxury				✗
Delta Queen Steamboat Co.	River	$$$	Mass Market			✗	
Disney Cruise Line	Traditional	$–$$	Budget to Mass Market		✗		
Holland America Line	Traditional	$$$	Upscale				
KD River Cruises of Europe	River & Canal	$–$$	Budget to Mass Market				✗
Norwegian Cruise Line (NCL)	Traditional	$$–$$$	Mass Market		✗		

Cruise Line	Cruise Category	Price*	Passenger Category	Target: Singles	Target: Families	Target: Seniors	Target: Adventurers
Premier Cruise Lines	Traditional	$	Budget Market		✗		
Princess Cruises	Traditional	$$$–$$$$	Upscale				
Radisson Seven Seas Cruises	Traditional & Expedition	$$$$	Upscale to Luxury				✗
Renaissance Cruises	Traditional	$$$$	Upscale to Luxury				
Royal Caribbean International	Traditional	$$–$$$	Mass Market				
Seabourn Cruise Line	Traditional	$$$$$	Luxury				
Silversea Cruises	Traditional	$$$$	Upscale to Luxury				
Special Expeditions	Expedition	$$$$	Upscale				✗
Windjammer Barefoot Cruises	Masted Schooner	$–$$	Budget to Mass Market	✗			✗
Windstar Cruises	Masted Schooner	$$$$	Upscale				✗

*Price Key: Average cost per person, per day:
$ = under $200 $$$$ = $401–$600
$$ = $201–$300 $$$$$ = $600 +
$$$ = $301–$400

Figure 2.5 **Cruise Chart.**

average price range, passenger category, and four specific target groups: singles, families, seniors, and adventurers.

A word of caution: this chart is a *general guide* only. For example, every cruise line company listed will certainly attract a broad range of passenger types (for example, singles, families, couples, and so on). If one or more target groups are checked, that means that the cruise line markets and wants to attract that specific type of passenger. If a cruise line markets evenly for all types of passengers, no target group is indicated on the chart.

Checkpoint 2.1 _____

The following are four typical client profiles. Refer to Figure 2.5 and list which cruise line(s) you would recommend. (In each case there may be several that you could recommend; list only the requested number.)

1. Mr. and Mrs. Anderson are planning their fifth cruise. They are looking for a unique and adventurous experience this time. They are upwardly mobile, which means that they both work hard and earn a good living. They want to go for a week and can spend up to $5,000 for both of them on this trip.

    What two cruise lines would you recommend?

    _____   _____

2. Bob Harper is taking his first cruise and will be traveling alone. He wants to be with people his own age who are also single. He is on a strict budget and doesn't want to spend more than $1,000 for a seven-day cruise.

    What cruise line would you recommend? _____

3. Mr. and Mrs. Adams are traveling with two children: Billy, who is four years old, and Sally, who is sixteen. This is their first cruise and they want to make it a family experience. They are average wage earners and have saved up for this trip over a period of years. They want to experience what a cruise ship is like.

    What three cruise lines would you recommend?

    _____   _____   _____

4. Mr. and Mrs. Tolland are both retired seniors. They have traveled around the world and are used to staying at the best hotels, eating the best foods, and drinking fine wines! They are looking for a cruise ship that can cater to their every whim.

    What cruise line would you recommend? _____

SPACE RATIOS: HOW BIG IS BIG?

An important consideration when selecting a cruise is the size of the ship. Many cruise clients are concerned about seasickness. The size of the ship is a factor when determining how much motion will be felt during the

```
┌──────────────────────────────────────────────────────────────────────┐
│                                                                        │
│   What's considered. . . .                                             │
│                                                                        │
│       A small ship?        Under 5,000 GRT (fewer than 150 passengers) │
│                                                                        │
│       A midsize ship?      Between 16,000–35,000 GRT (600–1,200 passengers) │
│                                                                        │
│       A large ship?        Between 35,000–65,000 GRT (1,200–2,000 passengers) │
│                                                                        │
│       A megaship?          Over 65,000 GRT (2,000 or more passengers)  │
│                                                                        │
└──────────────────────────────────────────────────────────────────────┘
```

Figure 2.6 How Big Is Big?

cruise. The largest ships rock the least; smaller vessels will experience more motion.

Size is also a factor when determining how spacious or crowded the ship will feel. If you are selling a megaship that holds more than 2,400 passengers, clients may envision waiting in long lines or constantly bumping into other passengers wherever they go. The concern isn't so much size but how much elbow room there will be for the passengers. Will the ship appear to be spacious, with few on board, or will it feel like Times Square on New Year's Eve?

The best way to measure the amount of elbow room or passenger space is to calculate the ship's *space ratio*. This will tell you how much space is occupied by one passenger if a full complement of passengers is sailing.

A total capacity of 2,400 passengers may seem like a lot of people, and it will be if the ship is small. But that many passengers on a ship of 75,000 gross registered tons or more won't seem crowded at all; in fact, because of the enormous amount of passenger space, passengers will feel as if they are sharing the vessel with just a few others at a time.

A ship's size is measured in *gross registered tons*, or *GRT*. Regardless of what the name implies, GRT is not a measurement of weight. It is a measurement of interior space available and accessible to passengers on board the ship. Passenger cabins, dining rooms, entertainment lounges, and promenade decks are included in the GRT; the galley, the bridge, the crew's quarters, and the engine room are not.

Key Point: One GRT equals 100 cubic feet of enclosed passenger space.

It doesn't mean very much to describe the size of a ship *only* in terms of its gross registered tonnage. What is important is the *space ratio*, or the ratio of GRT to the *standard passenger capacity* on board the ship. Standard passenger capacity is reached if all cabins are occupied with two passengers.

Key Point: The Space Ratio equals GRT divided by standard passenger capacity.

Let's look at an example. Carnival Cruise Lines' *Destiny* has a GRT of 101,000, its standard passenger capacity is 2,642.

Space ratio = 101,000 divided by 2,642
= 38

Is a space ratio of 38 good or bad? Well, the higher the better. The following guideline will help:

A space ratio of . . .	Is . . .
Below 20	Below average (very crowded)
21–28	Average
29–38	Spacious
38+	Very spacious (like being on a private yacht!)

Checkpoint 2.2

1. For each cruise ship, the GRT and standard passenger capacity is provided. Calculate the space ratio for each.

   a. *Cunard Countess*: GRT = 17,593; standard passenger capacity = 790. Space ratio is _____.

   b. *Delta Queen*: GRT = 3,280; standard passenger capacity = 174. Space ratio is _____.

   c. *Crystal Symphony*: GRT = 49,500; standard passenger capacity = 960. Space ratio is _____.

2. Use your answers from question 1 to answer the following:

   a. Which ship would seem very crowded? _____

   b. Which ship is average in space? _____

   c. Which ship is extremely spacious and yachtlike? _____

CHAPTER REVIEW

1. Name the four general categories of cruise ships.

   _____   _____

   _____   _____

2. For each client description, which one of the four cruise ship categories would you suggest?

a. A young couple, who have never cruised before and are on a budget.

_____

b. A well-traveled retired couple, looking for something different and more exotic, they want to learn about new places and cultures.

_____

c. Clients who want a slow-moving, relaxing voyage up and down the Mississippi to visit the old plantations.

_____

d. A young couple who want an informal, action-packed cruise where they can even help to sail the ship.

_____

3. Name one cruise line company that offers:

a. Family-oriented travel.

_____

b. Luxury where price is no object.

_____

c. Educational and expedition-style cruises.

_____

d. River cruises within the United States.

_____

e. Tall-masted schooners in upscale or luxury class.

_____

f. Traditional cruises for a wide cross-section of travelers.

_____

4. Several cruise ships are listed here, from highest to lowest GRT. The standard passenger capacity is provided for each. Calculate the space ratio for each ship (rounded up to the nearest whole number).

		GRT	Passenger Capacity	Space Ratio
a.	*Monarch of the Seas*	73,941	2,744	_____
b.	*Regal Princess*	70,000	1,596	_____
c.	*Celebration*	47,262	1,900	_____
d.	*Costa Allegra*	30,000	804	_____
e.	*Radisson Diamond*	19,000	354	_____
f.	*Royal Viking Queen*	10,000	212	_____
g.	*Stella Oceanis*	5,500	300	_____

5. Put the ships listed in question 4 in order from most spacious to least spacious in terms of their space ratios.

(1) _____   (5) _____

(2) _____   (6) _____

(3) _____   (7) _____

(4) _____

A Day at Sea 3

After completing Chapter 3, students will be able to:

- List eight items or services that are typically included in the cost of a cruise.

- List eight items or services that are not typically included in the cost of a cruise.

- Describe the major functions and responsibilities of 20 types of cruise staff members as they directly relate to passengers.

- Describe a standard tipping policy found on most cruise ships.

- Name and describe a minimum of eight types of passenger recreational and sport facilities found on most cruise ships.

- Locate and identify passenger accommodations and public facilities on a deck plan.

- Describe the dining procedure in terms of table assignments.

KEY TERMS

air/sea packages
balconied cabin
debarkation
embarkation
inside cabin
open seating
outside cabin
per diem
porthole

ports of call
pre- and post-tours
pullman berth
seating times
shore excursions
suite
table assignments
tenders

- Describe the difference between tendering and docking.

- Describe the process of booking shore excursions.

- Describe the steps involved during embarkation and debarkation.

INTRODUCTION

Some aspects of cruising are totally different from any other type of vacation. The most appealing feature of a cruise is that the vessel itself provides practically everything that a land-based vacation offers: accommodations, dining, entertainment, recreation, sports, and a full range of passenger services. In order to sell cruises effectively, a travel professional must have thorough product knowledge. Short of taking a cruise yourself, the best way to gain that knowledge is to study what a typical cruise ship looks like and what it offers in the way of passenger facilities and services.

In this chapter you will learn about accommodations on board a cruise ship in addition to the wide variety of recreational, sports, entertainment, and other passenger services. First, we will study what is and is not included in the cost of a cruise.

WHAT'S INCLUDED

An attractive feature of a cruise vacation is that practically everything is paid for up front. This is a major reason why cruise travel has the highest percentage of customer satisfaction compared to other types of vacation experiences. Practically everything is prepaid, so the client knows exactly how much money to bring for the extras; there will be no unhappy surprises such as running out of money midway through the vacation because of expenses the traveler did not anticipate!

Most cruise travelers purchase *air/sea packages*. These packages include the basic cruise plus round-trip airfare from selected home cities, round-trip transfers between the airport and the cruise ship, and baggage handling. *Pre-tour* and *post-tour packages* are also available as an option. They include hotel accommodations, transfers, and some sightseeing at selected hotels at either the beginning or the end of the cruise vacation.

Included	Not Included
Accommodations	Liquor/soft drinks
Meals	Shore excursions
Entertainment	Onboard shops
Recreational facilities	Beauty parlor/barber shop
Round-trip airfare (on air/sea packages)	Onboard spa: massage, sauna, fitness center
Transfers (on air/sea packages)	Laundry/dry cleaning
	Medical services
Tips (on some ships)	Tips (on most ships)

Cruise vacations have the highest percentage of customer satisfaction because they are almost totally inclusive. The average cost for an air/sea cruise package *per diem*, or per day, is between $200 and $250 per person. This may seem expensive, but when you consider all that is included—airfare, accommodations, meals, and entertainment—a cruise vacation offers high value for the money.

To illustrate the value of a cruise vacation, let's compare a typical seven-day Caribbean cruise vacation with a comparable seven-day Caribbean land-based resort vacation. The prices used in the comparison are based on average prices between a mass-market ship and a comparable land resort located on the island of St. Maarten. Prices are approximate only and are based on two adults traveling during the winter (the peak or most expensive season).

	Cruise	Land-Based Resort
Base price	$3,500	$2,600
Airfare	included	$1,400
Transfers	included	included
Meals	included	$ 900
Tips	$ 100	$ 200
Sightseeing	$ 200	$ 400
Entertainment	included	$ 200
Beverages	$ 200	$ 280
Miscellaneous	$ 100	$ 100
Total	$4,100	$6,080
Cost per day (per person)	$ 293	$ 434

CRUISE PRICES: WHO PAYS STICKER PRICE ANYMORE?

The full advertised cost of a cruise depends on two major factors: departure date and cabin category. The price printed in a general cruise brochure is like a sticker price on a car: it is established by the manufacturer and based on such things as the model and what options are included. When you're shopping for a car, how often do you pay the sticker price? Very rarely. There are end-of-year discounts, trade-in prices, and lots of other reasons why you rarely pay the full advertised price. You can say the same thing for cruises. Paying the full advertised price for a cruise is becoming more the exception than the rule. Most clients want to buy cabins at discounted prices.

What types of discounts are available and who offers them? Discounts are offered by the cruise lines themselves and by cruise-only agencies.

Cruise Line Discounts

Cruise lines offer deals to boost sales on certain cruise departures. Usually the better discounts are offered during off-peak periods, such as during the summer in the Caribbean. These discounts can represent a dollar value (as much as several hundred dollars off the price of a one-week cruise), or as much as 50 percent off the regular price. Many lines offer "early bird" booking programs that encourage people to pay in full within a short period of time after booking. Other incentives offered by cruise lines include free pre- and post-cruise land packages, "kids sail free" offers, and free cabin upgrades.

A popular type of discount is the *passenger alumni* program. These are discount cruise rates offered to passengers who have sailed previously with that particular cruise company. Special alumni prices are offered on selected cruise departures. This helps the cruise lines gain customer loyalty and thus increase repeat business.

Travel agents are informed of the many cruise deals being offered through travel trade publications, advertisements sent or faxed to the agency by cruise companies, and the Internet. It's just a matter of doing some research!

Cruise-Only Agencies

Within the past several years, cruise-only agencies have become a major force in the marketing and selling of cruises. These companies have found a niche—they only market and book cruise travel for the traveling public. Because their specialty is the cruise product and they can guarantee a higher volume of cruise business, these agencies negotiate special discounts with the cruise lines they represent.

Cruise-only agencies usually offer their discounts directly to the general public; as a rule, they don't offer these deals through the all-service travel agencies. Cruise-only agencies advertise their cruise bargins through ads placed in newspapers and magazines, through direct mail, and on the Internet. Figure 3.1 shows an example of a promotion offered by a major cruise-only agency on selected sailings on the Holland America Line ships MS *Ryndam* and MS *Noordam*. As you can see, these individual sailings offered more than 50 percent discount value on selected cabin categories.

Who's who on board

Cruise ships can have anywhere between 250 and 500 crew and staff members. The number of crew and staff members depends on the size and type of cruise vessel. Most members of the cruise staff never come into direct contact with passengers; they handle cargo, cleaning, painting, and maintenance duties during the cruise.

Holland America Line®

PANAMA CANAL

ONE WEEK SALE

13 DAYS • OCT. 1 - OCT. 14, 1997
LOS ANGELES TO FT. LAUDERDALE

MS RYNDAM
55,000 tons; 1,266 guests; Registry: Netherlands

ITINERARY

DATE	PORT
Oct. 1	Los Angeles, California
Oct. 2-3	At Sea
Oct. 4	Puerto Vallarta, Mexico
Oct. 5	At Sea
Oct. 6	Santa Cruz Huatulco, Mexico
Oct. 7-8	Cruising south en route to Panama
Oct. 9	Enter Panama Canal at Balboa
	Transit the Panama Canal
	Leave the Canal at Cristóbal
Oct. 10	At Sea
Oct. 11	Oranjestad, Aruba
Oct. 12-13	At Sea
Oct. 14	Ft. Lauderdale, FL

$1,269
Inside Catg. N Gty.
Retail $3,145

$1,519
Outside Catg. H Gty.
Retail: $3,755

Port Tax: $230
Air Add-Ons: LAX: $399; SFO/DFW: $449; ORD/JFK: $549

10 DAYS • OCT. 25 - NOV. 4, 1997
ACAPULCO TO ACAPULCO

MS NOORDAM
33,930 tons; 1,214 guests; Registry: Netherlands
Ship does not transit Canal. Optional shore excursion to Canal Zone.

ITINERARY

DATE	PORT
Oct. 25	Acapulco, Mexico
Oct. 26	At Sea
Oct. 27	Puerto Quetzal, Guatemala
Oct. 28	At Sea
Oct. 29	Puerto Caldera, Costa Rica
Oct. 30	Scenic Cruising Golfo Dulce
Oct. 31	Taboga, Panama
	Balboa, Panama Canal Zone
Nov. 1-2	At Sea
Nov. 3	Santa Cruz Huatulco, Mexico
Nov. 4	Acapulco, Mexico

$799
Inside Catg. M Gty.
Retail $1,945

$899
Outside Catg. G Gty.
Retail: $2,335

$999
Deluxe Catg. C Gty.
Retail $2,815

Port Tax: $115
Air Add-Ons: LAX: $639; SFO: $669; ORD: $549;
DFW: $449; JFK: $599

Pacific Ocean | Balboa | Miraflores Locks | Pedro Miguel Locks | Continental Divide | Gatun Lake | Gatun Locks | Cristóbal | Atlantic Ocean

Figure 3.1 **Promotion offered by a cruise-only agency.**

To understand who works on ships and what they do, think of a cruise ship as a floating hotel or resort. Similar amenities and services are provided for passengers on a cruise ship and for guests vacationing at a land-based resort. On most traditional cruise ships, management is organized into two groups. The ship's staff consists of the captain, the hotel manager, the chief engineer, and the chief officer. The hotel staff is headed by the hotel manager and consists of the cruise director, the food service manager, the purser, the physician, the chief housekeeper, and the beverage manager.

There are about a dozen or so key staff members who interact with passengers. Both you and your clients should know who they are and what they do!

Title	Responsibilities	Passenger Contact
These people don't charge for their services:		
Captain	Serves as master of the ship; in charge of the well-being and safety of all passengers and crew members.	Infrequent
Chief engineer	Deals with all technical aspects of running the ship.	Infrequent
Chief officer	Responsible for maintaining the physical condition of the ship, inside and out.	Infrequent
Hotel manager	Directly responsible for nearly all aspects of the passenger's comfort and guest services; oversees everything except the nautical and technical aspects.	Infrequent
Purser	Supports the hotel manager in all matters of administrative management, and supervises the activities of the front office such as money-related matters and passenger safety-deposit boxes.	Frequent
Chief housekeeper	Oversees the maintenance of all staterooms, public rooms, lounges, and bars.	Infrequent
Food service manager	Coordinates and directs the supply and operation of the ship's kitchen, dining room(s), and restaurant(s).	Infrequent
Beverage manager	Responsible for the service in all lounges and bars; also assists passengers in the planning of private parties or events on board the ship.	Infrequent
Cruise director	Supervises all passenger information and entertainment; serves as master of ceremonies during shows, revues, and other entertainment functions. Responsible for staff members, including hosts and hostesses, entertainers, and shore excursion staff.	Frequent
Cabin steward	Takes care of passengers' accommodations; cleans and makes up cabins.	Frequent
Deck steward	Takes care of passengers while they are on deck; serves drinks and distributes pool towels.	Frequent/ as needed
Host/male escort	Provides companionship to single women on board by conversing and dancing with them during day and evening functions (available on certain ships).	As needed

Dining-room staff—These people don't charge, but you usually have to tip at the end of the cruise:

Maitre d'	Supervises entire dining room; takes care of any special passenger requests such as birthday or anniversary cakes and changes in table/seating assignments.	As needed

Table waiter	Recommends items on the menu, takes meal orders, and serves food during all formal meals served in the dining room.	Frequent
Bus person (assistant waiter)	Serves as a table waiter in training; assists the table waiter by clearing the table, serving meals, and filling water glasses.	Frequent
Wine steward	Recommends and serves wine at the table upon request.	As needed

These people charge for their services:

Physician	Directs all medical services and provides medical care for passengers, officers, and crew. The ship physician may have one or more nursing assistants, depending on the size of the ship.	As needed
Beautician	Provides hair and beauty care for all passengers; on larger ships there may be several on staff.	As needed
Masseuse	Provides massages upon appointment.	As needed
Photographer	Takes pictures of passengers while on the ship and during shore excursions; passengers have the option to purchase the photos.	Frequent

TIPPING

Tipping is often a concern for most people who are taking a cruise for the first time. Whom to tip, when to tip, and how much to tip are frequent questions asked of the travel professional. Tipping is at the passenger's discretion; passengers should base the amount on the quality and level of service provided. Sometimes tips are given when services are rendered; at other times the total tip is given at the end of the cruise in one lump sum.

Passengers tip the following staff upon services rendered: bartenders, wine stewards (although they are sometimes tipped at the end), masseuses, and hairstylists or beauticians. The amount of the tip should be the same as if you were being provided the same service off the ship—approximately 10 to 15 percent of the cost.

Passengers tip the following staff at the end of the cruise in one lump sum: cabin stewards, table waiters, buspersons, and the maitre d'.

The most convenient policy is a *no-tipping policy*. A few cruise lines do not want or expect tips to be given to any members of the staff; tips are already figured into the cost of the cruise. Some of the cruise lines that have a no-tipping-required policy are Cunard (*Sea Goddess*), Seabourn Cruise Line, Windstar Cruises, Radisson Seven Seas Cruises, and Holland America Line.

Tipping guidelines are printed in cruise brochures. The following table shows a standard guideline to follow for a typical seven-day cruise.

ACCOMMODATIONS

Ship accommodations are called *cabins* or *staterooms*. Cabins are much smaller and compact than the standard hotel room; space on board a cruise ship is at a premium. Cabins come in all varieties, shapes, and sizes and differ from ship to ship. However, you should be familiar with what a typical cabin accommodation is like.

Cruise ships provide accommodations for one, two, three, and four passengers, called *single*, *double*, *triple*, and *quadruple occupancy*, respectively. Only specific cabins on board a ship are large enough and designed for a third and fourth passenger.

In most cases, cabins come equipped with twin beds. Third and fourth passengers are accommodated in upper or *pullman berths*; these beds are pulled down from the wall when in use. On the more recently built ships, some of the larger cabins offer queen- or king-size beds. Beds on board a

Figure 3.2 **Average outside cabin. Courtesy of Clipper Cruise Line.**

Figure 3.3 Suite accommodations showing sitting area and private verandah.

ship are always bolted to the floor and can be moved only by members of the ship staff. On newer ships, a twin-bed configuration can be changed to a double-bed configuration upon the passenger's request.

All cabins are equipped with private bath facilities: toilet, sink, and shower. More expensive accommodations will usually contain a combination bathtub/shower with a lot more space. Other standard items in all passenger cabins are one closet per passenger (small in comparison to hotel closets) and a vanity, makeup, or dressing table. Cabins are air-conditioned and have telephones, color television, and radio. Some of the newer and larger ships have their own television studio on board so that all ship's activities and entertainment, movies, and world news are broadcast directly into each cabin.

In addition to size, decor, and furnishings, the cost of a cabin depends on three general factors:

Figure 3.4 Cabin bathroom facilities with bathtub and shower.

A Day at Sea **37**

1. *Location*: Cabins on the higher decks and amidships are generally more expensive because of their better view and smoother ride, respectively.
2. *Inside versus outside*: Cabins with a porthole or window (outside cabins) are generally more expensive than cabins without a porthole or window (inside cabins).
3. *Private balcony or verandah*: Some outside cabins may have a private balcony or verandah and are generally more expensive.

There are four general types of cruise cabins: *suites, balconied cabins* (or cabins with private verandahs), *outside cabins,* and *inside cabins.* Keep in mind that these cabin types are shown for simplification only. As a rule, ships do not label their cabins and price categories in any particular way.

- *Suites* are the most expensive accommodation on board a ship. They consist of multiple sections that generally include a sitting area, one or two bedrooms, a small kitchen or kitchenette, a private bar, and a private verandah on ships that offer them. Some ships are all-suite accommodations such as Cunard's *Sea Goddess I* and *Sea Goddess II.*
- *Balconied cabins* are also in the deluxe category but are less expensive than suites. They are outside cabins that have their own private balconies or verandahs. These cabins are often larger and the furnishings and decor are more lavish and colorful than standard cabins.
- *Outside cabins* run a wide range of price categories on any particular ship. The one thing they have in common is either a round porthole or large window. Portholes and windows in passenger cabins do not open.
- *Inside cabins* are the least expensive accommodation on a ship. The one thing they have in common is that they are located in the interior section of the vessel; there is no porthole or window with a view to the outside. Inside cabins will have a setup and bed configuration similar to that of outside cabins in the same category.

In a cruise brochure, each price is indicated by cabin category; some ships have a dozen or more price categories. Categories are usually named

---

BUYER BEWARE!

Be careful when selecting outside cabins on certain ships. Lifeboats are sometimes mounted on the side of the ship and hang down to the deck below. These lifeboats often obstruct the view from some of the outside cabins on that deck. Passengers who pay a higher price for an outside cabin for the view will be unhappy if their view is of a side of a lifeboat! Many cruise lines identify outside cabins with obscured views in their brochures.

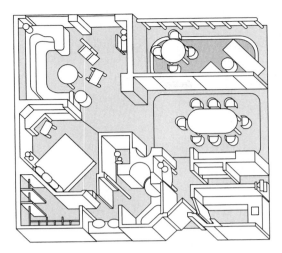

Figure 3.5 A typical suite.

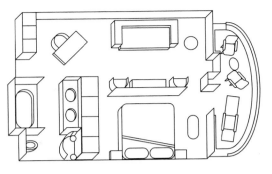

Figure 3.6 A typical balconied cabin.

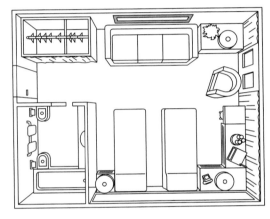

Figure 3.7 A typical outside cabin.

by letter: category A cabins are the most expensive, category B cabins are less expensive, and so on.

Cabins in one particular category may not be located together on the same deck; a category may consist of cabins located on two or more different decks. Why? Often there is a swap that can be made. For example, a small cabin located on the top deck may cost the same as a larger cabin located on a lower deck; the passenger is swapping a higher location for a larger cabin. Or a larger inside cabin may cost the same as a smaller outside cabin on the same deck; the passenger is swapping size for a window.

*F*INDING YOUR WAY AROUND: READING A DECK PLAN

The best way to find your way around any cruise ship is by a *deck plan*. A deck plan is a blueprint of a ship. It shows the location of cabins and all other passenger recreational and service areas. All cruise brochures and other resource material have printed deck plans. A deck plan can also be a vertical representation of a ship—the location of each passenger deck.

Refer to Figure 3.8, which shows deck plans for Princess Cruises' *Sky Princess*. This ship is 46,000 GRT with a passenger capacity of 1,200. A vertical cross-section identifying each passenger deck by name and location

SKY PRINCESS

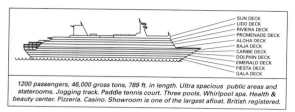

1200 passengers, 46,000 gross tons, 789 ft. in length. Ultra spacious public areas and staterooms. Jogging track. Paddle tennis court. Three pools. Whirlpool spa. Health & beauty center. Pizzeria. Casino. Showroom is one of the largest afloat. British registered.

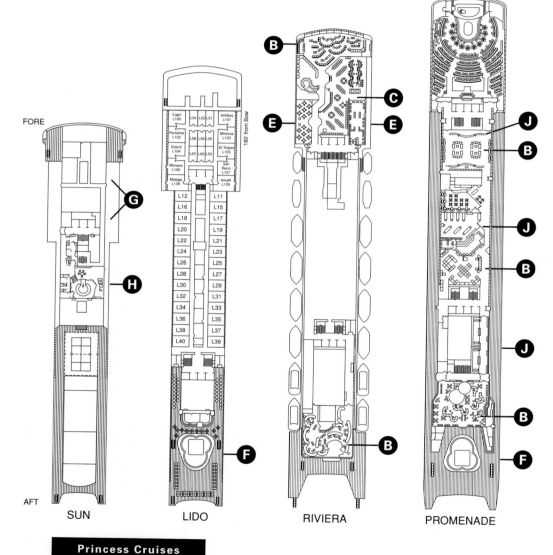

Figure 3.8 Deck plans for the *Sky Princess*.

DECK PLANS

- Distances listed are from the bow or stern to the nearest stateroom.
- All staterooms have two upper berths except where stateroom is marked with an asterisk (*). All staterooms have television.

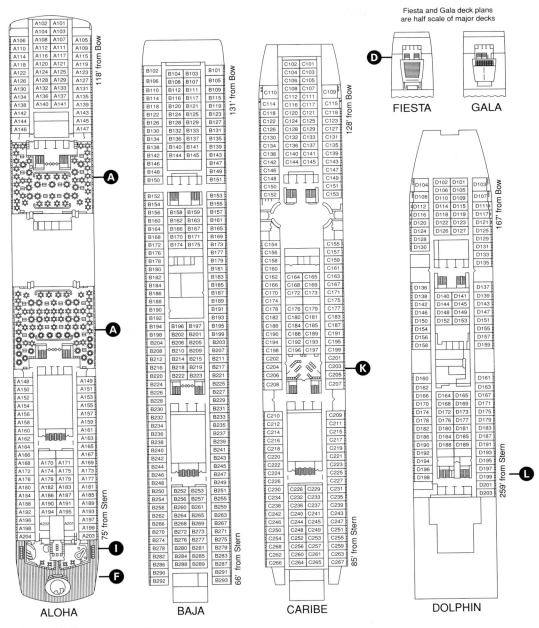

Fiesta and Gala deck plans
are half scale of major decks

FIESTA   **GALA**

ALOHA   BAJA   CARIBE   DOLPHIN

Figure 3.8 (continued)

appears at the top of the deck plan. The lowest passenger deck is called the Gala Deck. There are additional decks below Gala Deck, but they are restricted to crew only.

Refer to the deck plan and answer the following questions: (1) How many passenger decks does the *Sky Princess* have? (2) What is the name of the highest passenger deck? (3) What is the name of the main deck or the longest deck on the ship? (Right! Eleven, Sun Deck, and Aloha Deck.)

A deck plan can also be a *horizontal* representation of each separate deck on a ship. This provides a bird's-eye view of each passenger deck. The *Sky Princess* has eight full passenger decks. The deck plans identify the location of passenger cabins and suites and other entertainment and service facilities such as dining rooms, entertainment lounges, swimming pools, and shops.

Passenger cabins and suites are located on various decks on a ship. Cabins are identified by letters and numbers; suite accommodations are identified by names. On the *Sky Princess*, accommodations are located on these five decks starting from the highest: Lido, Aloha, Baja, Caribe, and Dolphin.

The cabins located on the same deck will begin with the same letter, the first letter in the name of the deck is used. For example, the cabins on the passenger accommodation deck, the Dolphin Deck, begin with the letter D. Cabins on the Caribe Deck, begin with the letter C; and so on.

Passenger suites are on the Lido Deck and are identified by both a number and a name. For example, a suite identified by the number L106 is also identified by the name Monaco Suite.

Cabin numbering can also help you figure out where the bow and the stern are located on a ship. Sometimes it isn't always obvious when looking at a deck plan! The general rule of thumb is that cabin numbers *increase from the bow to the stern*. There are exceptions to this, especially on smaller expedition ships and tall-masted vessels.

Inside cabins are identified easily, as they are located in the interior of the ship and not adjacent to any outside walls or bulkheads. For example, cabins B196 and B197 are inside accommodations on the Baja Deck. Can you identify the two inside cabins on the Caribe Deck that are located in the extreme bow section? (Right! C102 and C101.)

Outside cabins are adjacent to the outer bulkheads. For example, cabin numbers B180 and B181 on the Baja Deck identify two outside cabins that are located amidships. Can you identify the two outside cabin numbers on the same deck that are located aft? (Right! B292 and B293.)

Also notice that all even-numbered cabins are located on the same side and all odd-numbered cabins are on the other side. In our example, all even-numbered cabins are on the port side or the left side of the ship; odd-numbered cabins are on the starboard side or the right side of the vessel. This is different from ship to ship and should be checked in each case.

Checkpoint 3.1 _____

Refer to the *Sky Princess* deck plans (Figure 3.8) and answer the following questions.

1. Next to each cabin number, write *I* for an inside cabin and *O* for an outside cabin.

   _____ C178   _____ L21   _____ B252   _____ C131   _____ D165

2. Write the cabin number for each description.

   a. _____ An outside cabin, located on the Caribe Deck, starboard side, extreme aft section.

   b. _____ The inside cabin located on the Baja Deck, forward section, port side, closest to the companionway (inside stairs).

   c. _____ The outside cabin located next to and forward of cabin L38.

   d. _____ The number and name of the suite accommodation located on the Lido Deck, starboard side, extreme forward end.

A SHIP'S TOUR

In this section we will take you on a tour of a typical cruise ship—the shops, dining areas, sports areas, and recreational facilities. A ship is like a small town; it has something for practically everyone. You can watch spectacular Las Vegas–style entertainment, work out in the gym or fitness center, read quietly in the ship's library, or listen to a lecture about the next port of call.

To help you visualize our ship tour, we will refer you to Figure 3.8, the sample deck plan of the *Sky Princess*. Refer to this deck plan as you read through the descriptions that follow. Most of the passenger services and facilities described in this section of your text are cross-referenced by letter in Figure 3.8.

Dining (A on deck plan)

A major feature of any cruise vacation is dining on board—and there's a lot of it! Passengers are offered several opportunities throughout the day to dine: breakfast, midmorning snack, lunch, afternoon tea or snack, dinner, and a midnight buffet, in addition to 24-hour cabin service.

Formal meals—breakfast, lunch, and dinner—are offered in the ship's dining room, where meal times and seating are strictly regulated. Most cruise ships have a more informal, cafeteria-style restaurant or cafe, usually

Grand foyer on Carnival Cruise Lines' *Fantasy.*

located near the swimming pool area. Here passengers can eat breakfast or lunch more informally and at their leisure. Also, most ships provide self-service coffee and tea around the clock as well as buffets or pizza parties late at night! However, dinners are always served in the formal dining room. Figure 3.9 shows an example of a dinner menu.

Passengers' special dietary requirements, such as kosher or no-salt meals, should be requested in advance at the time of booking. In addition, most dining-room menus include "lean and light" items for health-conscious passengers who are looking for low-calorie and low-fat meals.

Dining-Room Assignments On most ships, dining-room hours and seating are strictly regulated. Passengers are not allowed to wander in at any time and sit anywhere

A bountiful feast during a midnight buffet.

Dinner

Apricot Nectar
Chilled Tomato Juice
Half Grapefruit Maraschino
Eggplant and Mushrooms, Riviera Style
Escargots de Bourgogne · Crab Meat Cocktail · Canapé de Foie Gras

✳ ✳ ✳ ✳ ✳

Cream of Shrimp au Sherry · Chilled Vichysoisse
French Onion Soup (Cheese Crouton)

✳ ✳ ✳ ✳ ✳

PARISIAN COQUILLE ST. JACQUES with Mixed Seafood, au Gratin.

CALF'S SWEETBREADS SAUTÉED GRENOBLOISE, Capers and Lemon.

COQ AU VIN, Chicken Parts, sealed, flamed with Cognac,
simmered with Onions and Mushroom in a hearty Burgundy Wine.

ROAST LOIN OF WESTERN PORK ROBERT, Julienne of Sour Pickles.

ROAST PRIME TENDERLOIN OF BEEF STRASBOURGEOISE, Goose Liver, Madeira Sauce

✳ ✳ ✳ ✳ ✳

Carrots Vichy · Artichoke Heart au Gratin · Petit Pois á la Française
Fondante Potato · Dauphine Potato

✳ ✳ ✳ ✳ ✳

Iceberg Pimiento
Caesar Salad · Health Salad
French · King and I · Thousand Island · Caesar

✳ ✳ ✳ ✳ ✳

Crisp Napoleon · Gâteau Paris Brest
Parfait Parisien · Soufflé Glacé Grand Marnier
Pineapple Sherbet · Cherries Jubilee

✳ ✳ ✳ ✳ ✳

Edam · Swiss · Gorgonzola · Cream
Camembert · Jarlsberg · Cream of Gruyére · Bel Paese
Port Salut · Cheddar

✳ ✳ ✳ ✳ ✳

Compote of Baked Apple
Fresh Fruit

✳ ✳ ✳ ✳ ✳

Sanka · Milk · Postum
Hot Chocolate
Coffee or Tea
Hot or Iced

Figure 3.9 **Example of a dinner menu.**

TYPICAL MEAL SERVICE

Time	Meal
6:45 A.M.	"Early bird" breakfast on deck
7:30 A.M.	Full breakfast buffet in lounge area
8:00 A.M.	Full breakfast menu in dining room
11:00 A.M.	Morning tea/bouillon and pastries on deck
12:00 noon	Buffet luncheon at poolside
12:30 P.M.	Full lunch menu in dining room
4:30 P.M.	Afternoon tea and snacks on deck
6:30 P.M.	Full dinner menu in dining room
12:00 midnight	Midnight buffet
24 hours	Food delivered to cabin at any time

they want during meal times. Some of the brand-new ships do offer restaurant-style dining; the majority of ships do not.

The *dining request*, made when booking a cruise, consists of two things: preferred *seating times* and *table assignments*.

Seating Times Since the main dining room on most cruise ships can accommodate only half of the passengers at a time, meals are served in two sittings—the *main* (or early) seating and the *second* (or late) seating. Seatings are usually 1½ to 2½ hours apart.

A typical dining room on a traditional cruise ship.

Seating times will differ from ship to ship. The times are printed in the cruise brochure for easy reference. On many ships, seating times only apply for dinner. They may have *open seating* during breakfast and lunch, which means that passengers may sit anywhere at any time during the posted times of the meal.

TYPICAL SEATING TIMES

Meal	Main Seating	Second Seating
Breakfast	7:00 A.M.	8:30 A.M.
Lunch	12:00 noon	1:30 P.M.
Dinner	6:00 P.M.	8:30 P.M.

Table Assignments   There are tables for two, four, six, eight, or ten people. Each passenger is assigned to a specific table number, depending on the table size requested.

> **Key Point:** Seating times and table assignments are only *requested* at the time of booking. The assignment is *confirmed* when the passenger boards the ship on the first day. It is also important to note that if passengers are unhappy with the seating time and/or table assignment, the maitre d' can usually change the seating time or table assignment if the dining room is not completely full. This should be taken care of on the first day of the cruise during embarkation.

Entertainment and Recreation

There is a wide variety of entertainment on board a traditional cruise ship; some ships have more than others. The variety and sophistication of theater, nightclub revues, stage performances, and variety shows vary from ship to ship. On the megaships (65,000+ GRT), there are numerous choices and some of the stage performances are on a professional level.

Passengers receive a daily schedule each night that lists all of the next day's scheduled events, tours, shows, dining hours, and other useful information. The daily schedules are delivered to the cabins in the early evening. Figure 3.10 is a sample daily schedule from Carnival Cruise Lines.

Bars, Lounges, and Nightclubs (B on deck plan)   Depending on the size and type of cruise ship, there can be anywhere from one to several different bars and lounges scattered throughout the vessel. Prices are comparable to what you pay on land. The minimum drinking age is the standard, 18, however, on a ship it is always at the captain's discretion. Liquor purchased in bars, lounges, and nightclubs on board a ship is not typically included in the price of the cruise; it is a pay-as-you-pour system.

Each ship will have a main entertainment lounge or showroom that schedules nightly entertainment. Everything goes, from magic shows to

M.S. ECSTACY		SATURDAY, DAY 7
6:20 AM	Coffee & Danish	Panorama Grill — Lido
7:00 AM – 8:00 PM	Nautica Spa & Gym Opens	Sports Deck Forward
7:00 AM	Walk-A-Mile	Olympic Track — Sun Deck
7:30 AM	Stretch & Relaxation	Aerobics Studio
7:45 AM	Breakfast — Main Sitting	Both Dining Rooms
8:00 AM	Slot Machines Open	Crystal Palace Casino
8:00 AM – 8:00 PM	Nautica Spa Salon Opens	Sports Deck Forward
8:00 – 10:00 AM	Light Deck Breakfast	Panorama Grill — Lido
8:30 AM	Low Impact Aerobics	Aerobic Studio
9:00 AM	Breakfast — Late Sitting	Both Dining Rooms
9:00 AM – 8:00 PM	Galleria Shopping Mall Opens	Atlantic Deck
9:30 AM	Dynaband® Calisthenics	Aerobics Studio
9:30 AM – 8:00 PM	Video Diary Desk Opens	Empress Deck
9:30 AM	Bridge Walk-Through	Meet Portside — Lido Deck
10:00 – 11:00 AM	Coffee, Tea & Bouillon	Panorama Grill — Lido
10:00 AM	Trapshooting	Promenade Deck Aft
10:00 – 11:00 AM	Library is Open	Explorer's Club
10:00 AM	Horse Racing	Blue Sapphire Lounge
10:30 AM	Aqua Aerobics	Verandah Deck Aft
11:00 AM	Photo Gallery Opens	Empress Deck Grand Atrium
11:00 AM	Senior Aerobics	Aerobics Studio
11:30 AM – 2:30 PM	Light Lunch & Salad Bar	Panorama Grill — Lido
11:30 AM – 2:00 PM	Specialty Sandwiches	Lido Deck Poolside
11:50 AM	Captain's Bulletin from the Bridge	
12:00 NOON	Lunch — Main Sitting	Both Dining Rooms
12:00 NOON	Full Casino Opens	Crystal Palace Casino
1:00 PM	Ice Carving Demonstration	Lido Deck Poolside
1:30 PM	Lunch — Main Sitting	Both Dining Rooms
2:00 – 3:00 PM	Library is Open	Explorer's Club
2:00 PM	Trapshooting Tournament	Promenade Deck Aft
2:00 PM	Ping Pong Tournament	Verandah Deck
2:45 PM	Newlywed & Not-So-Newlywed Game	Blue Sapphire Lounge
3:00 PM	Bingo	Blue Sapphire Lounge
4:00 PM	Multi-Impact Aerobics	Aerobics Studio
4:00 – 5:00 PM	Ice Cream & Cookies	Lido Grill — Outside
4:00 – 5:00 PM	Frozen Yogurt	Lido Grill — Inside
4:00 – 5:00 PM	Tea Time	Society Bar
4:30 PM	Masquerade Parade	Blue Sapphire Lounge
5:00 – 6:00 PM	"Fun Ship" Highlight Party (Main)	Metropolis Bar
6:00 PM	"American" Dinner Main Sitting	Both Dining Rooms
7:00 – 8:00 PM	"Fun Ship" Highlight Party (Late)	Metropolis Bar
7:30 –8:30 PM	Farewell Party for Teens & Jr. Cruisers	Stripes Disco
8:00 PM	"American" Dinner Late Sitting	Both Dining Rooms
9:00 PM	Super Trivia	Blue Sapphire Lounge
9:00 PM	Sweet Music	Society Bar
9:30 PM	Bingo	Blue Sapphire Lounge
9:30 PM	Listen to "Sea Breeze"	Starlight Lounge
9:30 PM	Piano Bar Opens with "Scott"	Neon Bar
9:45 PM	Music Society Plays	Chinatown
10:00 PM	Disco Opens with "Jeff"	Stripes Disco
12:30 – 1:30 AM	Quiche & Salad Buffet	Wind Song Dining Room
1:30 – 2:00 AM	Mini Buffet	City Diner — Promenade Deck

DRESS FOR THE EVENING: Casual.   MOVIE: "Regarding Henry" 7:30, 10:00 AM, 12:30, 3:00, 5:30, 8:00, 10:30 PM, 1:00, 3:30 AM

Figure 3.10 **Sample daily schedule from Carnival Cruise Lines.**

full-stage performances that include singers, comedians, dancers, and audience participation. On some of the bigger ships, full Broadway-style shows or Las Vegas revues are surprisingly sophisticated and extravagant full-scale productions.

Casinos (C on deck plan)   Once a cruise ship is in international waters (twelve miles off shore), passengers are permitted to gamble. Most cruise ships will have casino facilities; some are more sophisticated than others. In fact, the cruises marketed "to nowhere" cruise just far enough out into international waters to permit gambling; the main attractions are gambling and evening entertainment.

On smaller and older ships, the casino may consist of several slot machines. On the larger and most recently built ships, casinos offer full service, including poker, baccarat, blackjack, roulette, craps, and slot machines.

Movie Theaters (D on deck plan)   Almost all ships, except for the smallest vessels, have at least a separate room that functions as a screening room or a full-size cinema-style theater. Films that are shown are a few months or more from the general release date. A different film is usually featured each night of the cruise and some ships may have two or more showings during the day.

On many of the newer ships, each passenger cabin comes equipped with a television and a VCR. Passengers can help themselves to the ship's video library and view current movies and other performances at any time from the comfort of their cabins.

Library and Game Rooms (E on deck plan)   Most cruise ships offer library facilities; some have a small collection of a few dozen books, while others

Ship's casino on a traditional cruise ship.

have up to 1,500 volumes (or more) consisting of best sellers, reference books, and magazines. Many ship libraries also stock videotapes. There is no charge for borrowing books and magazines, although a small refundable deposit may be required.

Card rooms with card tables and board games are also found on most ships. This is the area where passengers engage in private card and board games and compete in tournaments of such games as bridge, canasta, and chess. In addition, family-oriented cruise ships may also offer small video arcades and computer learning centers.

Sports and Fitness

Our society places a lot of importance on maintaining a healthy lifestyle: eating the right foods, exercising, and losing weight. Cruise ships want to make their passengers feel comfortable by providing them with many of the same activities and amenities that they get at home. On board a cruise ship, athletic types can join exercise and aerobics classes, work out in the gym, or jog around a specially designated weather deck. Health-conscious passengers can listen to lectures on eating right, reducing stress, lowering cholesterol, and losing weight. Taking a cruise today no longer means non-stop eating and a sedentary lifestyle. For passengers who want it, there is ample opportunity to enforce a healthy lifestyle while on a cruise vacation.

Swimming Pools (F on deck plan) One or more swimming pools is a standard feature on most cruise ships. Some of the larger vessels feature two large pools and a small wading pool for children; some have indoor pools in addition to those on deck.

Pool deck amidships on the *Galaxy*.

Fitness center and gym on the *Royal Majesty*.

Pools are not large enough for long-distance laps but can be very elaborate, with water slides and retractable roofs. Pools can be filled with either saltwater or fresh water. There are no lifeguards on duty and pools are emptied or covered with canvas during rough weather and while in port.

Sports Deck (G on deck plan)   This top deck, also called the sun deck, contains many different sports and recreational facilities. In addition to one or more pools, this area may include deck sports such as volleyball, paddle tennis, driving ranges, shuffleboard, or table tennis.

Exercise/Fitness Rooms (H on deck plan)   Fitness centers on cruise ships can range from a small room on a lower deck to an airy, sunny, glass-enclosed space on the top deck with a sweeping view of the sea. Fitness centers offer such services as sauna and massage (which usually cost extra), and sophisticated exercise equipment for the passengers. These services should be reserved a day or two in advance. On newer ships, walking and jogging tracks are located on the uppermost sun or sports deck, away from passenger sleeping accommodations.

Most ships have a full-service exercise room with up-to-date

> ## WATCH OUT FOR WATER HAZARDS!
>
> Royal Caribbean International's *Legend of the Seas* and *Splendour of the Seas* feature eighteen-hole golf courses on each of their top decks! This is not just miniature golf: each course measures approximately 7,000 square feet, complete with winding fairways, sand bunkers, and water hazards!

bodybuilding equipment, stationary bicycles, motorized treadmills, stretching machines, aerobics classes, and personal fitness lectures or private consultations. Many cruise ships offer structured physical fitness programs that last throughout the length of the cruise, free of charge. They often include lectures on fitness, nutrition, and weight loss, and are often tied in to a special spa menu offered in the dining room.

Passenger Services

Youth Facilities (I on deck plan)   Many cruise lines market their ships for the entire family, and children of all ages are welcome. Some ships provide more things for children to do than others; you should check it out in each case. Ships that target families offer structured activities day and night for children of all ages. In fact, they are kept so busy with planned activities that children and their parents may be together only during meals in the dining room! Figure 3.11 shows a sample children's activity schedule.

FUN, FACTS, AND FIGURES!

Have you ever wondered how much it takes to feed nearly 2,000 passengers during a one-week cruise? Below are the store supplies on the cruise ship *Galaxy* for an average seven-day cruise. The Galaxy is 77,713 gross registered tons and carries approximately 1,800 passengers.

21,600	pounds of beef		2,500	pounds of rice
5,040	pounds of lamb		1,500	pounds of cereal
3,360	pounds of pork		600	pounds of jelly
2,520	pounds of veal		1,650	pounds of coffee
1,680	pounds of sausage		1,600	pounds of cookies
4,200	pounds of turkey		42,000	tea bags
11,760	pounds of fish		30	pounds of herbs and spices
675	pounds of crab		3,400	bottles of assorted wines
3,250	pounds of lobster		200	bottles of champagne
21,500	pounds of fresh vegetables		200	bottles of gin
2,500	pounds of potatoes		290	bottles of vodka
16,800	pounds of fresh fruit		350	bottles of whiskey
2,500	gallons of milk		150	bottles of rum
250	quarts of cream		45	bottles of sherry
600	gallons of ice cream		600	bottles of assorted liqueurs
8,650	dozen eggs		10,100	bottles/cans of beer
4,200	pounds of sugar			

KIDS' CRUISE NEWS

Welcome to your First Day at Sea   MONDAY

7:30–9:30 A.M.   Breakfast—open sitting .... Windows on the Sea Restauant

****

9:00 A.M.   For all you early birds, it's your chance to see how the ship
                is controlled by the captain and his officers! Meet on Promenade.

10:00 A.M.   Mandatory boat drill to be attended with your parents!

10:30 A.M.   All kids . . . meet on Promenade! Your chance to learn how to make
                balloon animals and how to juggle!

11:30 A.M.   Lunch time! Meet for lunch in the Reflections Lounge and we will go
                to the Signals Cafe together.

12:30 P.M.   Open swim! Join your new friends at the Topsiders poolside!

2:30 P.M.   Hula hoops, tinikling sticks and peacock feathers . . . Come and join
                us in the theater for lots of fun!

3:30 P.M.   Draw Our Cruise Director Contest! Join us on the Promenade to draw
                Danny Corbeille!

4:00 P.M.   Face painting! Meet on Promenade to have your face painted!

4:30 P.M.   Message in a bottle! Let's write a message, put it in a bottle, and
                throw it overboard! Meet on Promenade!

4:00–5:00 P.M. Children's tours sign-up time! Parents, please sign up your child at this time
                at the shore Excursion Desk!

5:00 P.M.   It's charade time! Meet in the Signals Cafe!

5:15 P.M.   Early sitting—Passengers captain's gala champagne party!
                Your chance to join parents to meet the captain!

5:30 P.M.   Games and more games! Meet in the Signals Cafe for all kinds
                of card and board games!

7:30 P.M.   Late sitting—Passengers captain's gala champagne party!
                Your chance to join parents to meet the captain!

7:30 P.M.   Sea monster drawing contest! Draw the ugliest, scariest, funniest
                sea monster you can think of! Meet in the Signals Cafe!

Norwegian Cruise Line

Figure 3.11 Kid's Cruise News.

JOIN MICKEY AND THE GANG ON DECK!

A revolutionary concept in family cruising has evolved with the advent of Disney Cruise Line. The ship *Disney Magic* embarks from Port Canaveral, Florida. What's so special? It is the first cruise line that caters to family travel. In fact, there is an entire deck exclusively for children. According to the Disney Cruise Line brochure, "A large staff of friendly, well-trained Disney counselors help [children] explore 15,000 square feet of space dedicated exclusively to kids" (more than ten times that of most other ships).

The children's areas on board the ship are imaginative, with such fun names as the Oceaneer's Lab, Buzz Lightyear's Cyberspace Command Post, and the Animator's Palate—a lively dining room where the whole room changes from black and white to colorful animation by the end of the meal!

The entire vacation consists of a three- or four-day theme park stay at Disney World, and a three- or four-night cruise on the *Disney Magic*. The seven-day vacation includes round-trip airfare from selected cities, ground transfers, a three- or four-day stay at either a moderate or a deluxe resort located inside Disney World, and all admissions to the nine theme parks within the huge Disney World resort complex. Prices range from budget to moderate, depending on which Disney property is selected in Disney World.

During the cruise portion, the ship embarks from Port Canaveral and visits Nassau, Bahamas, and Castaway Cay, a private island reserved for the *Disney Magic* and its passengers.

To find out whether a ship is family-friendly, check for the following services and amenities that most such cruise ships provide: children's playrooms and youth centers with professional counselors, structured activities each day, special discos and electronic game rooms, and ice cream and pizza parlors.

Shops and Photo Gallery (J on deck plan) Depending on the size of the ship, there may be one or two stores that offer everything from toothpaste to sweatshirts, or a multi-tiered mall-like shopping center chock-full of specialty stores and boutiques. Stores on ships are duty-free; in addition to standard personal items, they include fine jewelry, gift items, liquor, and fashionable clothes. In fact, Cunard's *Queen Elizabeth II* features a seagoing branch of London's famous Harrods department store.

Choices of merchandise are limited on board the ship. However, since items are purchased duty-free, prices are slightly lower than for the same items purchased on land.

Every ship will also have a photo shop to one degree or another. Photos are taken by the ship's photographers, who seem to be everywhere on

Shops and boutiques on Celebrity Cruises' *Galaxy.*

the cruise! They snap pictures of passengers from the time they board up to the day before the end of the cruise. All pictures are placed on display for viewing and passengers may select those they wish to purchase. Each photo can cost anywhere from $4 to $15, depending on the size.

Beauty Salon/Barbershop (K on deck plan) Smaller ships may offer one hairdresser on staff for both men and women. Larger ships usually offer a complete beauty parlor with a separate barbershop for men. This service is available by appointment and a nominal fee is charged; the cost is similar to prices at a local salon.

CASHLESS SOCIETY

Passengers don't have to carry cash around with them during the cruise. Passengers are given a ship's charge card that is used for all purchases on board the ship. The card is used to purchase drinks in all bars and lounges, items in shops, shore excursions, and so on.

The ship's charge card is validated by a major credit card number provided by the passenger. At the end of the cruise, the total purchases are totaled and paid automatically by the passenger's credit card. Passengers also have the option of paying the final bill by cash or traveler's check at the end of the cruise.

Medical Services (L on deck plan)   Cruise ships will have, at the very least, one doctor on board. Larger ships offer fully equipped infirmaries, staffed with several doctors and nurses. Passengers can visit the ship's doctor during scheduled office hours, or cabin visits can be arranged if necessary. Fees for office visits can range anywhere from $20 to $40 per office consultation plus whatever medication is needed.

Standard medical insurance policies are not accepted on board the ship. However, passengers may submit medical bills to their insurance companies for reimbursement after arrival home.

Over-the-counter remedies such as aspirin or seasickness pills can be obtained directly from the purser's office; the passenger does not need to visit the ship's doctor for minor ailments.

Room Service   The level of cabin service differs from ship to ship. On smaller, expedition-style vessels, room service may be restricted to the ship's doctor visiting an ailing passenger. Most traditional-style cruise ships offer 24-hour cabin service from limited breakfast, lunch, and dinner menus at no extra charge except for such items as beer, liquor, or wine.

Dry Cleaning and Laundry   Laundry service is offered on all but the smallest ships and may consist of a self-service laundry, full-service laundry, or a combination of both. Valet service, where both laundry and dry cleaning are picked up and delivered back to the passenger's cabin is available on most traditional cruise ships. Valet service usually takes about 24 hours and there is a charge for each garment or piece of laundry.

Observation lounge on the Clipper Cruise Line.

Religious Services Most cruises that last a week or more offer some type of worship service for their passengers. Services are mostly interdenominational on Sundays and during holidays. Some ships offer Catholic masses and Friday evening Jewish services. The type of service depends upon the cruise area and/or country of registry. Religious services are held in such rooms as the ship's library, the theater, or one of the passenger lounge areas.

The seemingly endless weather deck on Norwegian Cruise Line's megaship *Norway*.

Going ashore

Now that you have some idea of what happens on board cruise ships during days at sea, let's take a look at what happens when the cruise ship is in port.

Tendering versus Docking

When the cruise ship arrives at a port of call it either docks at the pier or drops anchor off shore. The decision to dock or drop anchor depends on any one or all of these factors:

- the size of the ship
- space available at the pier
- weather conditions

If the ship docks at the pier, it pulls up alongside the dock area. Passengers debark or leave the ship by walking down the gangway, which extends from the side of the ship to ground level.

If the ship anchors off shore the passengers debark or leave the ship by riding small boats or *tenders* to shore. Tenders usually accommodate 100-200 passengers at one time. They will sail back and forth continually between the ship and shore while the ship is at anchor.

A Day on Land

While the cruise ship is in port, passengers have four options:

- purchase a *shore excursion/land tour*
- arrange their own tour
- walk around on their own
- do nothing and stay on board the ship!

A popular option for most passengers is to purchase one or more *shore excursions*. Shore excursions usually include land transportation from the ship, a narrated tour, sightseeing led by local guides, and sometimes a meal or snack. Some shore excursions may be just scheduled transportation to and from the major beach or shopping areas.

Usually a shore excursion is either a half day (3–4 hours) or a full day (6–8 hours). For lengthy cruises to places like the Middle East or the Orient, overnight land accommodations may be included in the shore excursion. For example, a popular shore excursion on an Eastern Mediterranean cruise is a trip up the Nile River to visit Cairo and points further south. Because of the distance covered, an overnight stay in Cairo is included.

Shore excursions are not part of the cruise fare; they are always extra. They usually cannot be purchased before the cruise, but are confirmed and paid for during the cruise. The exception to this applies to lengthy, international cruises through Europe, the Middle East, or the Far East, for example. Since land options sometimes have to be arranged and confirmed far in advance with the local ground operators in foreign countries in these areas, passengers have the option of reserving and paying for shore excursions before they depart. The best policy is to check with the cruise line regarding its policy on shore excursions.

Figures 3.12 and 3.13 are reprints of two shore excursions in Mexico and the Caribbean, respectively. In addition to the duration and price, shore excursion descriptions include the sights and attractions, the method of transportation, and the amount of walking or activity involved.

TAXCO
SHORE EXCURSION
SATURDAY

TOUR ACA-6   **ONE DAY TRIP**

You will depart from the dockside at 6:30 A.M. to begin the gradual ascent from the lush tropical growth at sea level to majestic sights of mountain vistas and verdant areas under cultivation in the temperate zone. In Chilpancingo (the state capital of Guerrero), stop for a continental breakfast (orange juice, coffee, and sweet rolls). From there, you will continue through the Valley of Candelabras (majestic cactus plants) and see Vulture Canyon; all the while, your guide will explain the sights and give you some of the history and lore of the area. In Taxco, you will see silver that has been handcrafted into jewelry and other objects; you will also see other handicrafts for which the region is noted. Vista Santa Prisca Church (an architectural masterpiece) and stop for a sumptuous lunch at the Bonanza Restaurant. You will have time for shopping and more sightseeing before starting the return trip back to the ship. On the way back, you will stop again in Chilpancingo for refreshments. We recommend you wear your most comfortable walking shoes, and take a sweater or jacket along for the cooler climate in the higher altitude. Don't forget your camera!

Duration: 14 hours   Per Person: $125.00
by motorcoach   Leave Pier: 6:30 A.M.

Figure 3.12 Shore excursion in Mexico.

ST. THOMAS
SHORE EXCURSION
WEDNESDAY

Passengers are met shipside by the famous *Kon-Tiki* raft. This is the tour renowned for its free-flowing rum punch barrels and its reputation of being the Caribbean's best (and sometimes the wildest) party tour.

Starting slowly with the steel band playing calypsos of the islands, the *Kon-Tiki* cruises gently through the bustling harbor of Charlotte Amalie. The captain points out the castles and forts and places of interest while photographers find the open upper deck an ideal vantage point. Passing behind the island in flat calm waters, *Kon-Tiki* pauses for a while over a beautiful coral reef, where she lowers her four large glass-bottomed viewers for everyone to see the wonderful variety of corals, sponges, and tropical fish. Proceeding into Honeymoon Bay, *Kon-Tiki* gently kisses the beach and holds herself there with a line to a coconut tree. A stairway is lowered for everyone to disembark to swim or laze in this beautiful palm-fringed cove (four changing rooms aboard).

With everyone back on board it's really party time from there on. The band quickens the tempo, the crew joins in, and soon everyone is dancing. A conga line leaves everyone exhausted and while some catch their breath the others top up their glasses, a "Name That Tune" contest is held, with winners receiving a bottle of the famous *Kon-Tiki* rum punch.

Duration: 2½ hours   Per Person: $30.00
Departure: 1:45 P.M.   Min: 40

Figure 3.13 Shore excursion in the Caribbean.

Checkpoint 3.2 _____

1. Describe the two types of dining-room assignments that are made by the travel agent at the time of booking.

   _____   _____

2. When are dining-room assignments confirmed?

   _____

3. Can dining-room assignments be changed? If so, when and how?

   _____

4. Your clients, the Flynn family, are thinking of going on a cruise for the first time as a family vacation. Their main concern is boredom—since they will be spending three days at sea, they are afraid there isn't going to be much for them to do! What would you say to them to overcome their concern? (Mention at least five specific examples in your explanation.)

   _____

   _____

   _____

   _____

5. Explain what is meant by "a cashless society" on board a cruise ship.

   _____

   _____

6. List three reasons why a ship would have to drop anchor rather than dock at a port of call.

   _____

   _____

   _____

7. What is the name of the small boat that carries passengers between the ship and shore when the ship is at anchor?

   _____

8. _____ True or false: Shore excursions are usually included in the cost of the cruise.

9. _____ True or false: Shore excursions are not usually paid for in advance.

10. What is the difference between docking and anchoring at a port of call?

    _____

Embarkation and Debarkation Procedures

Embarkation is the process of boarding the ship on the first day of the cruise. *Debarkation* is the process of leaving the ship on the last day of the cruise. Embarkation and debarkation will often leave people feeling apprehensive and unsure of what they are supposed to do. The standard procedure that is followed by all cruise ships is described in this section in a question-and-answer format. *Q* stands for the client's question and *A* is the travel agent's response.

Q: *What time do we board the ship when we first arrive?*

A: Passengers are not allowed to board the ship before the published embarkation time. Most cruise ships have only several hours of turnaround time. Turnaround is the amount of time needed to drop off passengers and their luggage at the end of one cruise; board new passengers, luggage and supplies; and set sail for the next voyage. This is all done within the space of several hours.

   Most ships will dock at the end of a cruise early in the morning, around 6 or 7 A.M. If the ship is scheduled to sail late that afternoon or early evening, standard embarkation time for newly arriving passengers begins around 1 or 2 P.M. Embarkation times differ from ship to ship and usually depend on such factors as the size of the ship, the port facilities, and other administrative matters such as immigration and customs clearance. Embarkation times are printed in cruise brochures for easy reference.

Q: *We are flying to Miami (the port of departure) on the day of arrival. How do we get from the airport to the ship? Will someone be meeting us when we get off the plane?*

A: If the passenger is on an air/sea package, round-trip transfers between the airport and ship are included. Passengers are met by a cruise line representative upon their arrival. Passengers are then transported to the ship and their luggage is delivered automatically to their cabin. Independent passengers must make their own arrangements by taxi or other public transportation. All cruise lines maintain desks in baggage-claim areas and will assist in transferring passengers and their luggage from there.

Q: *Do we tip anyone along the way?*

A: If the passenger is on an air/sea package, tips are already included. If the passenger is arriving independently, a standard tip to the taxi driver is recommended. Passengers' baggage is given to a porter at dockside, who then transports it to the ship; you should tip about $1 per bag to the porter.

Q: *What happens when we check in for our cruise? Do we go through security like at the airport?*

A: Passengers check in for the cruise at dock side before entering the ship. Cruise officials will ask for the cruise ticket and will inspect or even retain the passenger's official identification, such as a passport or certified birth certificate, at that time. Passengers also are required to pass through a security check and to pass hand-carried luggage through an x-ray inspection, in a procedure similar to airport check-in procedures.

Key Point: It is important to emphasize that all documents be available at this time: cruise ticket and proof of citizenship.

Q: *What happens when we board the ship for the first time?*

A: The ship's photographer takes pictures as the passengers board for the first time. Passengers have the option to purchase the photo during the cruise. Passengers are then greeted by a cruise staff member and escorted to their cabins by stewards. On small vessels, passengers receive their cabin key from a cruise officer and are directed to the cabin. Luggage is transferred to the cabin, it normally takes about one to two hours for delivery.

Q: *What's happening on the ship during embarkation?*

A: When the ship is in dock, nothing much is open on board the ship. Shops, casinos, pools, and other passenger service areas remain closed. However, a light buffet is usually served to arriving passengers in a designated area on board the ship.

Each passenger's table assignment confirmation is usually left in the cabin. This assignment shows the seating time (early or late) and the assigned table number. Passengers who wish to change their dining arrangements can see the maitre d', who is stationed in the dining-room area.

Ship's charge cards for passengers are distributed at this time and imprints are made of the passengers' personal credit cards, on which the total amount of cruise expenses is charged at the end of the cruise.

Q: *What happens during debarkation at the end of the cruise?*

A: Debarkation is a relatively simple process. A passenger briefing usually a few days before the end of the cruise explains debarkation. Passengers are asked to leave their packed luggage outside their cabins before they go to sleep or by a designated time (usually around midnight). When the ship docks, luggage is transported off the ship onto the pier.

It is important to remember *not* to pack what you intend to wear the next day, as it's not a good idea to leave the ship in your pajamas! Also remember not to pack airline tickets and other important documentation needed to exit the ship.

When the ship docks, it normally goes through one or two hours of immigration and customs clearance. When this is completed, passengers are allowed to leave the ship. Once passengers are off the ship, they must identify their luggage, which by this time is lined up in a waiting area at the pier. For air/sea passengers, luggage is transferred to the airport and checked in for the return flight.

Independent passengers must retrieve their luggage and obtain public transportation. In many cases, the cruise line offers transfers at a nominal fee for independent passengers traveling to the airport.

CHAPTER REVIEW

1. List four things that are always included on a cruise:

   _____   _____

   _____   _____

2. List two additional features (besides those listed in question 1) that are included in an air/sea package:

   _____   _____

3. List five items/services that are usually not included in the cost of the cruise and must be purchased while on board:

   _____   _____   _____

   _____   _____

4. Explain why cruise vacations offer a superior value.

   _____

   _____

5. What is the difference between an outside and an inside cabin?

   _____

6. Identify a potential problem when selling an outside cabin.

   _____

7. What is the most expensive type of acccommodation on board a cruise ship?

   _____

8. How soon after passengers first board the ship will their luggage arrive?

   _____

9. Name three cruise staff members who are usually tipped at the end of the cruise:

   _____   _____   _____

10. Name three cruise staff members who are usually tipped when services are rendered:

    _____   _____   _____

11. List three types of passenger services found typically on cruise ships:

    _____   _____   _____

12. List three factors that affect the cost of a cabin:

    _____   _____   _____

13. Circle the amount that comes closest to what two people would pay in tips to the following staff members at the end of a four-day cruise: cabin steward and dining room-staff.

    a. $95.00   c. $25.00
    b. $64.00   d. $125.00

14. True or false: All cabins in one cost category will be located on the same deck and will be the same size. Explain your answer.

    _____

    _____

15. _____ True or false: Most shops and the casino will remain open while the ship is in port for those passengers not taking a shore excursion.

16. Are overnight land accommodations ever included in the price of a shore excursion? If so, when?

_____

17. What does _open seating_ mean? When does it usually apply?

_____

_____

18. Match each staff member with his or her main responsibility.

a. cabin steward

b. captain

c. busperson

d. maitre d'

e. cruise director

f. purser

g. deck steward

h. table waiter

i. host

_____ Recommends menu items and serves meals in the formal dining room.

_____ In charge of passenger entertainment; serves as master of ceremonies at all functions.

_____ Brings towels and drinks at poolside.

_____ In charge of all money matters.

_____ Assists in dining room, clears table, and fills water glasses.

_____ Converses and dances with single women on board.

_____ In charge of the formal dining room.

_____ In charge of everyone's safety and well being during the cruise; master of the vessel.

_____ Takes care of passengers' accommodations.

Use the deck plan in Figure 3.14 to answer questions 19–30.

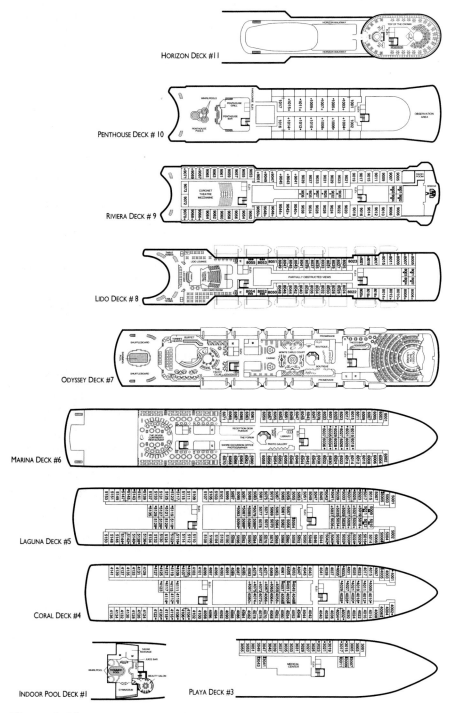

Figure 3.14

19. This ship has ten passenger decks. Which three decks do not have passenger cabins.

_____   _____   _____

20. Which is the lowest deck for passenger accommodations?

_____

21. Which is the highest deck for passenger accommodations?

_____

22. How many swimming pools does this ship have? _____

Which decks have a pool? _____

23. On which deck is the casino located? _____

24. What is the name of this ship's dining room (restaurant)?

_____

25. Your clients want an outside cabin. Both outside cabins 8036 and 6048 are available for the same price. Which one has the better value? Why?

_____

_____

26. Which of these cabins is located one deck below and directly under the dining room?

5151   5056   6070   5121   6065

27. On which deck are the medical facilities located?

_____

28. What is the name of the ship's main showroom?_____

On which deck is it located? _____

29. Which statement *does not* describe the location of the ship's shops?

a. forward of the casino   c. two decks above the dining room
b. aft of the showroom   d. same deck as the outside pool

30. Circle the cabin number below that best describes each of the following requests.

a. Outside, port side, aft on the Coral Deck.

4123   4001   4114   4141   4134

b. On the same deck as the dining room, forward, starboard side.

6056   6007   6070   6004   6001

c. Aft of the bridge, outside, starboard side.

9036   9001   9004   9008   9030

Itineraries 4

After completing Chapter 4, students will be able to:

- Name and identify a minimum of six popular cruise itineraries within the Western Hemisphere.

- Name and identify a minimum of six popular cruise itineraries within the Eastern Hemisphere.

- Locate and label the following major embarkation points and ports of call in the Western Hemisphere:

Acapulco	Bermuda
Fort Lauderdale	Juneau
Honolulu	Miami
Los Angeles	New Orleans
Nassau	San Juan
San Francisco	St. Thomas
Sitka	

KEY TERMS

Alaska Inside Passage	Mexican Riviera
Amazon River	Panama Canal Transit
Coastal China and Japan	port-intensive
Eastern Caribbean	repositioning
Eastern Mediterranean	Southern (Deep) Caribbean
Galápagos Islands	Western Caribbean
inland waterways	Western Mediterranean

WORLD CRUISE AREAS

"Where am I going?" This question is likely to be asked, along with "What is the ship like?" and "How's the food?" In fact, often the itinerary of the ship is the first factor when selecting a cruise.

You would be amazed to find out to which places on earth you can cruise: the common or traditional cruise itineraries, such as the Caribbean, the Bahamas, and the Mexican Riviera, and less traditional itineraries such as trips to Antarctica, the Galápagos Islands, or the Far East. First we will familiarize you with the major cruise itinerary areas of the world. Let's start with a map of the world and see where these areas are located. Figure 4.1 shows the following major cruise areas of the world:

Alaska	Hawaii
Amazon River	Indian Ocean
Antarctic Peninsula	Inland rivers of North America
Australia/New Zealand	Inland waterways of Europe
Baltic	Mexican Riviera
Black Sea	New England and Maritimes
British Isles	Nile River
East Atlantic	Orient
East Indies	South Pacfic
Eastern Meditteranean	Southeast Asia
Eastern/Southern Caribbean	Western Caribbean
Fjords	Western Meditteranean

And yes, your clients can even take a slow boat to China!

By the way, there are more cruise areas than are listed here! We have not included cruises to Bermuda and around South America on the map.

The most popular cruise areas that you should become familiar with include the Western Caribbean, the Eastern Caribbean, the Southern Caribbean, Mexico, and Alaska. Caribbean cruises, by far, are the most popular in the world. *That is why Miami, Florida, is the busiest cruise port in the world.*

WESTERN HEMISPHERE CRUISES

The majority of American first-timers cruise to destinations within the Western Hemisphere: the United States and Canada, the West Indies, Mexico, and South America.

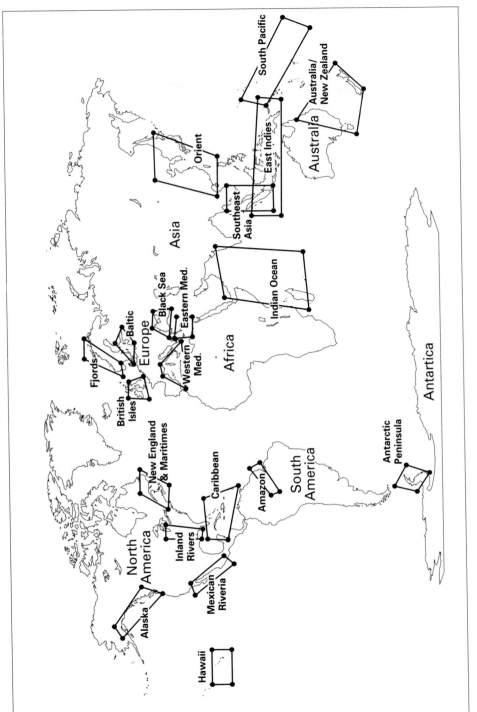

Figure 4.1

United States and Canada

In the United States, two popular itineraries are offered year-round: Mississippi riverboats and cruises to Hawaii.

Mississippi River   Nostalgic riverboat cruises on the Mississippi evoke what it was like to travel on the opulent paddle-wheelers of the past. During the warmer summer and fall months, these riverboats concentrate on northern itineraries, visiting such ports as Minneapolis–St. Paul and St. Louis. During the cooler months, the southern port cities of New Orleans and Memphis are key gateways used to tour the old Southern plantations and antebellum mansions. The Delta Queen Steamboat Company operates three ships: the *Delta Queen*, the *Mississippi Queen*, and the *American Queen*, which is the largest passenger steamboat ever built.

Hawaii   The other year-round cruise destination is Hawaii. The only major cruise company registered in the United States, American Hawaii Cruises, schedules weekly sailings that embark from Honolulu on the island of Oahu, with stopovers on Maui, Kauai, and the big island of Hawaii.

These cruises are *port intensive*; they visit a new port of call each day. American Hawaii Cruises also has the distinction of offering the most shore excursions at each port of call.

Alaska   Alaska is the fastest-growing cruise destination in North America. The Alaska cruise season is short; it begins in May and ends in early October. Many consider Alaska trips a cruise to "the last frontier" and the ultimate travel experience.

On Alaskan cruises, emphasis is placed on spectacular scenery as ships sail through towering fjords and offer close-up views of awesome glaciers. Passengers get a glimpse of interesting sea life, including whales, seals, and leaping dolphins. Land animals such as elk, bear, and moose can also be viewed from the comfort of deck chairs. These cruises also include a glimpse of native Alaskan cultures with side trips to native villages and historical sites in places such as Juneau, Ketchikan, Skagway, and Sitka.

Cruise ships that sail Alaskan waters often combine optional land-based motorcoach and rail tours to the interior. Holland America Line and Princess Cruises operate many ships in this area.

West Indies and Mexico

The most popular cruise destination in the world is the West Indies. This includes seasonal sailings to Bermuda and year-round cruises to the Bahamas and the Caribbean islands. The entire Caribbean is divided further into three cruise regions: the *Eastern Caribbean*, the *Western Caribbean*, and the *Southern* or *Deep Caribbean*. These terms are used in cruise brochures and other literature for marketing purposes.

Eastern Caribbean cruises include the ports of Freeport and Nassau, Bahamas; San Juan, Puerto Rico; and St. Thomas, U.S. Virgin Islands. Embarkation is usually from the ports of Miami and Fort Lauderdale. Because of the close proximity of the ports of call to the embarkation points, these cruises can be as short as three days or up to seven days in length.

Western Caribbean cruises concentrate on the Yucatán Peninsula in Mexico, with visits to the island of Cozumel and the beach resort of Playa del Carmen on Mexico's mainland. Caribbean destinations on these cruises include Grand Cayman and Jamaica. The major ports of embarkation for Western Caribbean itineraries are Miami and Tampa; they usually include a short stopover at nearby Key West, Florida.

Southern or *Deep Caribbean* cruise itineraries include ports that are located in the southernmost Caribbean, as far south as the South American ports of Caracas, Venezuela, or Cartagena, Colombia. The major embarkation port is San Juan, Puerto Rico, which places the cruise ship in the heart of the Caribbean. This positioning reduces the number of days needed to sail to and from the first and last port of call. These cruises are port-intensive because there are fewer days at sea and more days visiting ports of call.

Mexican Riviera cruises concentrate on the western or Pacific coast of Mexico. The Pacific coast is generally considered to be the "Riviera" of Mexico because many popular vacation resorts are located here. Major ports of embarkation for these cruises include Los Angeles and San Diego, California, or Acapulco, Mexico. These year-round cruises can be taken either round-trip or one way in either a northbound or southbound direction. Popular ports of call include the resorts of Cabo San Lucas, Mazatlán, Puerto Vallarta, Zihuatanejo, and Acapulco.

Panama Canal cruises include the best of both worlds: the Caribbean and the Mexican Riviera. They also include the interesting 50-mile journey by water between the Caribbean and the Pacific through the Panama Canal. A canal guide boards the cruise ship when it enters the first lock and narrates a running commentary about the canal's history, construction, and operation throughout the ten-hour daytime transit. Some ships will include only a partial transit; they pass the first lock and cruise Lake Gatún before exiting through the same lock. Other ships offer ten- to fourteen-day one-way full-transit journeys in either an eastbound or westbound direction. Panama Canal cruises include ports of call in the Caribbean and Central America and along the Mexican Riviera. However, cruise ships that transit the canal will rarely stop in the country of Panama itself.

South America

South American cruises offer a wide variety of sights and experiences for both first-time and repeat cruisers. There are four general cruise regions of South America: *eastern* and *western coastal*, *Amazon River*, *Galápagos*, and *Antarctica*.

Along the eastern coast, the three key ports of call are Río de Janeiro, Montevideo, and Buenos Aires. Along the western coast, the key ports are Callao (the port for Lima, Peru) and Valparaíso (the port for Santiago, Chile).

South America offers many choices for more adventurous travelers. Amazon River cruises operate seasonally from the chief port of Manaus, Brazil. Another adventure choice would be a scientific exploration by ship to the Galápagos Islands, which are protected environments off the coast of Ecuador. Passengers fly from the gateway of Quito, Ecuador, to the Galápagos Islands, from where cruise ships embark.

Perhaps the ultimate cruise adventure is the ice-breaker cruises to Antarctica. Ships embark from various ports in Chile and Argentina for the incredible voyage to the "bottom of the world."

Figure 4.2 is a quick, at-a-glance chart of major Western Hemisphere cruise itineraries. Use it as a handy resource tool.

EASTERN HEMISPHERE CRUISES

The Eastern Hemisphere offers many scenic, adventurous, and exotic cruise destinations. This part of the world is more appealing to the repeat or seasoned American cruise traveler.

Europe

The continent of Europe, because of its geography, offers some of the greatest opportunities for cruising. Europe is made up of a series of islands and peninsulas, which results in a lengthier coastline than most people would expect. Many capitals and major cities are located on or near the European coastline, making them easily accessible to cruise ships. Many other cities and points of interest are located on navigable rivers found throughout the continent.

European cruises can be placed in the following general categories: the Mediterranean, the Atlantic coast, the Scandinavian peninsula, inland waterways, the Black Sea, and the Baltic Sea.

Mediterranean itineraries include both western and eastern routes. *Western Mediterranean* cruises include ports in southern and eastern Spain, southern France, Italy, the island of Malta, and even some northern African ports in Tunisia and Morocco. *Eastern Mediterranean* itineraries include ports in Greece, the former Yugoslavia, and coastal Turkey, with an emphasis on Middle Eastern destinations in Egypt, Israel, and Cyprus.

Scandinavian itineraries can be divided into two major areas: the Baltic Sea and the fjords. Copenhagen is the primary port of embarkation for both Baltic and fjord cruises. Baltic Sea cruises offer a glimpse into the life and

CRUISE AREA	EMBARKATION/ DEBARKATION	TIME OPERATING	PORTS OF CALL	LENGTH
UNITED STATES AND CANADA				
Alaska	Vancouver, San Francisco, Seattle	May–October	Juneau, Skagway, Ketchikan, Sitka, Inside Passage, Glacier Bay	7–14 days
Atlantic Coast	Halifax, New York City, Boston, Fort Lauderdale, Savannah	May–October	St. Simons Island, Hilton Head Island, Charleston, Halifax, Boston, Newport, New York, Baltimore	7–14 days
Hawaii	Honolulu	Year-round	Kauai, Maui, Hilo and Kona on Hawaii	3–7 days
Mississippi River	New Orleans, St. Louis, Memphis, Minneapolis– St. Paul	Summer/fall (northern Mississippi); winter/spring (southern Mississippi)	Baton Rouge, St. Francisville (Louisiana); Natchez, Vicksburg (Mississippi)	2–10 days
WEST INDIES AND MEXICO				
Bahamas	Miami, Port Everglades, Port Canaveral	Year-round	Bermuda, Nassau, St. Thomas, San Juan	3–7 days
Bermuda	Boston, New York, Philadelphia, Baltimore	May–October	Bermuda	7 days
Eastern Caribbean	Miami, Tampa, Port Everglades, San Juan	Year-round	Nassau, Freeport (Bahamas); San Juan; St. Thomas	7 days
Southern or Deep Caribbean	San Juan	Year-round	St. Maarten, Antigua, Barbados, Martinque, Aruba, Caracas	7 days
Western Caribbean	Miami, Tampa, Port Everglades	Year-round	Grand Cayman, Jamaica, Mexican ports of Cancún and Cozumel	7 days
Panama Canal	Acapulco, San Juan, Miami, Fort Lauderdsale	Year-round	Costa Rica; Cristóbal, San Blas Islands (Panama); Cartagena, Colombia	7–14 days
Mexican Riviera	Los Angeles, San Francisco, Acapulco	Year-round	Cabo San Lucas, Mazatlán Puerto Vallarta, Acapulco	3–7 days
SOUTH AMERICA				
South America— east and west coasts	Acapulco, Buenos Aires, Los Angeles, Miami, Río de Janeiro	December–April	Montevideo (Uruguay); Río de Janerio (Brazil); Buenos Aires (Argentina); Lima (Peru); Valparaíso (Chile).	7–60 days
Amazon River	Manaus (Brazil)	November–February	Belém, Santarém (Brazil)	4–7 days
Antarctica	Puerto Williams, Punta Arenas (Chile); Buenos Aires (Argentina)	October–February	Beagle Channel; Port Stanley (Faulkland Islands); Antarctic Peninsula; Strait of Megellan; Cape Horn	10–30 days
Galápagos Islands	Quito, Guayaquil	Year-round	Galápagos Islands	3–10 days

Figure 4.2 Major western hemisphere cruise itineraries.

culture of such countries as Sweden, Finland, Russia, Germany, and Poland. Scandinavian fjord cruises emphasize the grandeur of the mountainous coastline for which Norway is famous. A *fjord* is a steep and narrow valley with an opening to the sea. The highlight of these cruises is the experience of being on a huge seagoing vessel as it slowly sails through the steep and narrow cliffs of the fjords.

Black Sea cruises offer a more exotic view of Europe. Primary embarkation ports are Piraeus (the port for Athens, Greece) or Istanbul, Turkey. These itineraries offer a view of intriguing destinations such as the city of Varna and the Golden Sands resort in Bulgaria; Constanta in Romania; and Odessa and Yalta in Ukraine. Black Sea itineraries combine the historical importance of ancient Greco-Roman era with the modern-day culture and folklore of Eastern Europe.

Europe's Atlantic coast embraces a wide area from the Canary Islands off the coast of North Africa to the ports along the North Sea. Some of the popular cruise areas in this part of Europe include (1) the Madeira and Canary Islands off the coast of North Africa; (2) the western coast of the Iberian Peninsula, including ports in Portugal and Spain; (3) the western coast of France and the Low Countries of Belgium and the Netherlands; and (4) the British Isles, with ports of call in England, Scotland, Wales, and Ireland. European coastal cruises range from seven to fourteen days in length and are sometimes combined with ports in other cruise areas such as the Western Mediterranean.

Europe's inland waterways consist of hundreds of miles of rivers and canals that wind through some of the most beautiful scenery on the continent. Small riverboats, deluxe barges, and chartered yachts take cruise passengers deep into the interior regions of Europe—where larger traditional cruise ships cannot go.

European river cruises are dominated by the Rhine and Danube, which transport passengers through some of the most beautiful scenery in the heartland of Europe—France, Germany, Austria, and Hungary, for example. Barges and chartered yachts navigate the smaller rivers and canals in Western Europe. Some of the most popular itineraries include the wine regions of France, the historic centers of Belgium and the Netherlands, and the quaint countryside of Great Britain.

Pacific Rim

Another important cruise area is the Pacific Rim. This huge area includes eastern and southern Asia, Australia, New Zealand, and many South Pacific islands. This part of the world is fast becoming a major destination for cruise ships. The most popular itineraries include coastal China and Japan, southeast Asia, East Indian islands, Australia, and South Pacific islands.

Coastal China and Japan cruise itineraries open up one of the most mysterious and exotic regions of the world to the cruise traveler. Cruises to this part of the world usually exceed fourteen days and sail as far north as Tokyo, Japan, and Beijing, China, to as far south as Hong Kong. Cruises are usually one-way in either a northbound or southbound direction. Because of the geography and location of major sights, shore excursions are always included.

Beijing is an example of a land-only portion. Beijing, the capital city of China, is located approximately 100 miles from the coast. Cruise ships stop at Tianjin, the port for Beijing, where cruise passengers debark and are transported by motorcoach to the city of Beijing. Passengers are provided with accommodations, meals, and sightseeing during a two- or three-day stopover in Beijing before returning to the ship. In addition, Coastal China and Japan itineraries include stops in Shanghai, Nanjing, and Hong Kong, plus a cruise up the Yangtze River into China's interior. Japan is also included on these cruises, with a stop in Osaka where the historic cities of Nara and Kyoto are visited.

Southeast Asia itineraries include visits to Vietnam, Thailand, Singapore, and Malaysia. Cruise ships embark from Hong Kong, Singapore, or Bangkok; cruises are usually fourteen days or more in duration. This region is relatively new to cruise travel, which provides easy access to destinations that have been difficult to visit in the past. Some of the unique ports of call include Da Nang and Ho Chi Minh City in Vietnam.

East Indies itineraries emphasize the countries of Indonesia and Malaysia, which are made up of thousands of islands and extend from the South Pacific to the Indian Ocean. Major destinations include the island of Bali; Jakarta, Indonesia; and the exotic country of Brunei. Because this region is located along the equator, it has the potential of becoming a popular winter cruise destination for North American travelers.

The continent of *Australia* and the many islands of the *South Pacific* afford a vast and ideal area to explore by ship. Itineraries in Australia include

---

REPOSITIONING: A SPECIAL WAY TO CRUISE

Some cruise ships make seasonal changes to their itineraries during the year. For example, a cruise company may operate a ship in the Caribbean during the winter season, and in the Mediterranean during the summer months; the ship is being *repositioned* from the Caribbean to Europe. Or, another ship may cruise Alaska during the summer season and reposition to the South Pacific during the winter and spring. Rather than sail without passengers and therefore suffer a loss of revenue, cruise lines market these repositionings as special cruises for passengers. Repositioning cruises often include exotic or interesting ports of call along the way and usually exceed fourteen days in duration. They are especially attractive to travelers who have a lot of time and who are looking for a different and unique cruise experience.

the ports of Sydney, Brisbane, and Cairns, which is the gateway to the Great Barrier Reef. Some cruises combine Australia with stops in New Zealand, including the cities of Auckland and Wellington in northern New Zealand and the mountains and fjords in the southern region. Extended cruises from either Australia or New Zealand include visits to some of the more exotic South Pacific islands, such as Fiji, American Samoa, and Tahiti in French Polynesia.

Figure 4.3 is a quick, at-a-glance chart of the major Eastern Hemisphere cruise itineraries.

EUROPE AND MIDDLE EAST				
Western Mediterranean	Genoa, Venice, Lisbon	May–October	Rome, Florence, Naples, Monaco, Nice, Barcelona, Palma de Majorca, Málaga, Cádiz	10–14 days
Eastern Mediterranean	Piraeus (port for Athens, Greece), Venice	May–October	Corfu, Istanbul, Kusadasi, Cyprus, Ashdod, Haifa (Israel), Alexandria, Port Said (Egypt)	7–14 days
Scandinavia/ Baltic	Copenhagen, Tilbury (port for London)	June–September	Stockholm, Helsinki, St. Petersburg, Tallinn, Riga, Gdynia, Rostock, Berlin (Gemany)	7–14 days
Scandinavia/ Fjords	Copenhagen, Oslo, Tilbury	June–September	Bergen, Trondheim, Tromso, North Cape	10–14 days
Black Sea	Istanbul, Piraeus	June–September	Istanbul, Odessa, Yalta, Constanta (Romania), Varna (Bulgaria)	7 days
PACIFIC RIM				
Coastal China and Japan	Osaka (Japan); Hong Kong (China)	October–April	Shanghai, Tianjin (port for Beijing), Nanjing, Yangtze River	14 days
Southeast Asia	Hong Kong, Bangkok, Singapore	November–April	Da Nang, Ho Chi Minh City (Vietnam), Phuket (Thailand)	14–22 days
East Indies	Singapore, Jakarta	December–May	Bali, Surabaya (Indonesia), Brunei	14–22 days
Australia and South Pacific	Sydney	December–May	Cairns, Brisbane (Australia), Auckland, Wellington (New Zealand), Fiji, American Samoa, Papeete (Tahiti)	14–22 days

Figure 4.3 **Major eastern hemisphere cruise itineraries.**

The following pages present a close-up view of some typical cruise itineraries. For each, a brief description along with a map showing major ports of call is presented. A sample day-to-day itinerary is also reproduced for each region.

Eastern Caribbean

Eastern Caribbean cruises are four and seven days long and embark from either Miami or Fort Lauderdale. Seven-day cruises usually include two or three days at sea. Most of the major cruise lines either own or lease a small uninhabited island in the Caribbean that they use as a port of call. Passengers have the option of spending a day on a deserted island with many of the same amenities found in an island resort; food, drinks, dancing, sports, and entertainment are provided by the ship.

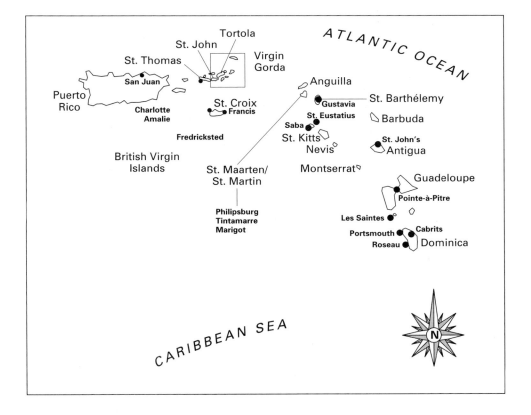

Figure 4.4

Day	Port	Arrive	Depart
7-DAY CRUISE ON ROYAL CARIBBEAN **INTERNATIONAL'S _SOVEREIGN OF THE SEAS_**			
Saturday	Miami		5:00 P.M.
Sunday	At sea		
Monday	Labadee, Haiti _(ship's private resort)_	8:00 A.M.	3:30 P.M.
Tuesday	San Juan	1:30 P.M.	
Wednesday	San Juan		1:30 A.M.
	St. Thomas	7:00 A.M.	4:00 P.M.
Thursday	At sea		
Friday	Cococay, Bahamas	1:00 P.M.	6:00 P.M.
Saturday	Miami	8:30 A.M.	

Western Caribbean

Western Caribbean cruises are usually seven days long and embark from Miami, Fort Lauderdale, or Tampa. This itineray includes some of the Western Caribbean islands such as the Cayman Islands, Jamaica, and Cozumel, and the beach resort of Playa del Carmen in Mexico. Passengers like this itinerary because it combines the beaches and shopping of major Caribbean resort islands and educational trips to the Mayan ruins in Mexico's Yucatán region.

Tendering in the Caribbean.

Figure 4.5 Western Caribbean ports of call.

7-DAY CRUISE ON CARNIVAL CRUISE LINES' *IMAGINATION*

Day	Port	Arrive	Depart
Saturday	Miami		4:00 P.M.
Sunday	At sea		
Monday	Playa del Carmen*	7:00 A.M.	7:30 A.M.
Monday	Cozumel	9:00 A.M.	
Tuesday	Cozumel		12:00 P.M.
Tuesday	At sea		
Wednesday	Grand Cayman	7:30 A.M.	4:30 P.M.
Thursday	Ocho Rios, Jamaica	8:00 A.M.	3:30 P.M.
Friday	At sea		
Saturday	Miami	8:00 A.M.	

*Operational stop for Tulum tour debarkation only.

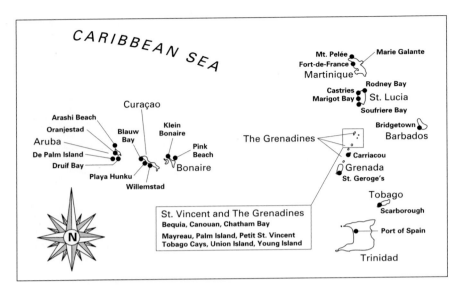

Figure 4.6

Southern (Deep) Caribbean

Southern Caribbean cruises have more ports of call than Eastern and Western Caribbean itineraries. These cruises are port-intensive because most of them embark from San Juan, Puerto Rico, in the heart of the Caribbean, which saves time sailing to and from the coast of the United States during the cruise, allowing fewer days at sea and more days in port. Southern Caribbean itineraries include many of the islands south of St. Maarten. This string of islands is called the Lesser Antilles. Itineraries are anywhere from seven to ten days long and usually include a stop as far south as northern

7-DAY CRUISE ON CELEBRITY CRUISES' *ZENITH*			
Day	**Port**	**Arrive**	**Depart**
Saturday	San Juan		11:30 P.M.
Sunday	St. Thomas	7:00 A.M.	5:00 P.M.
Monday	Guadeloupe	9:00 A.M.	4:30 P.M.
Tuesday	Grenada	8:00 A.M.	4:30 P.M.
Wednesday	La Guaira	10:00 A.M.	6:00 P.M.
Thursday	Aruba	7:00 A.M.	6:00 P.M.
Friday	At sea		
Saturday	San Juan	9:30 A.M.	

South America: either La Guaira (port of Caracas, Venezuela), or Bogotá, Colombia.

Bermuda

One-week cruises to Bermuda provide four days in port and three days at sea. The number of cruise lines serving Bermuda is limited due to the time each ship spends in port and the size of the island and its harbors, and also because unlike the Caribbean, Bermuda is a seasonal port of call—the cruise season begins in April and ends in October. Most ships embark from New York or Boston. It should be noted that Bermuda-only cruises do not embark from Florida because of the distance. Bermuda is sometimes combined with another port of call, such as the Bahamas. In this case, Florida is the most likely embarkation port.

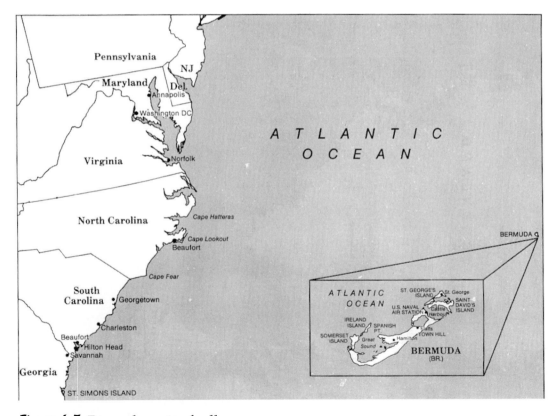

Figure 4.7 Bermuda ports of call.

7-DAY CRUISE ON NORWEGIAN CRUISE LINES'
NORWEGIAN MAJESTY

Day	Port	Arrive	Depart
Sunday	Boston		4:00 P.M.
Monday	At sea		
Tuesday	St. George's, Bermuda	10:00 A.M.	
Wednesday	St. George's		
Thursday	St. George's		
Friday	St. George's		1:00 P.M.
Saturday	At sea		
Sunday	Boston	8:00 A.M.	

View from the starboard side on the cruise ship *Norwegian Crown*: Rounding a tight corner through the Norwegian fjords.

Mexican Riviera

The western coast of Mexico, called the Mexican Riviera, includes major ports of call such as Cabo San Lucas, Mazatlán, and Puerto Vallarta. Cruises are either round-trip or one way between Acapulco and Los Angeles, San Diego, or San Francisco.

Figure 4.8 Mexican Riviera ports of call.

7-DAY CRUISE ON CARNIVAL CRUISE LINES' *JUBILEE*			
Day	**Port**	**Arrive**	**Depart**
Sunday	Los Angeles		4:00 P.M.
Monday	At sea		
Tuesday	At sea		
Wednesday	Puerto Vallarta	8:00 A.M.	10:00 P.M.
Thursday	Mazatlán	9:00 A.M.	6:00 P.M.
Friday	Cabo San Lucas	7:00 A.M.	Noon
Saturday	At sea		
Sunday	Los Angeles	9:00 A.M.	

Panama Canal

Panama Canal cruises allow passengers to experience the best of both worlds—the Caribbean and the Mexican Riviera—and the unique passage between the two oceans. It takes one full day to transit the canal, which is done during daylight hours for maximum effect. Cruises can be taken either in a westbound direction (from the Caribbean to the Pacific) or an eastbound direction (the Pacific to the Caribbean). Cruises can take up to two weeks and can originate and terminate in Los Angeles or San Francisco or even as far north as Vancouver, Canada.

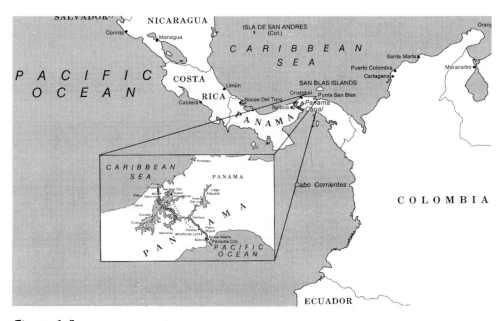

Figure 4.9 Panama Canal ports of call.

Transiting the Panama Canal—view from the bow.

15-DAY CRUISE ON CELEBRITY CRUISES' *GALAXY*

Day	Port	Arrive	Depart
Sunday	Fort Lauderdale		4:30 P.M.
Monday	At sea		
Tuesday	Cozumel	8:00 A.M.	4:00 P.M.
Wednesday	Grand Cayman	1:00 P.M.	7:00 P.M.
Thursday	At sea		
Friday	Panama Canal	7:00 A.M.	4:00 P.M.
Saturday	At sea		
Sunday	Puerto Caldera	7:00 A.M.	7:00 P.M.
Monday	At sea		
Tuesday	At sea		
Wednesday	Acapulco	8:00 A.M.	6:00 P.M.
Thursday	At sea		
Friday	Cabo San Lucas	9:00 A.M.	6:00 P.M.
Saturday	At sea		
Sunday	San Diego	9:00 A.M.	6:00 P.M.
Monday	Los Angeles	8:00 A.M.	

Alaska

Alaska cruises have dramatically increased in numbers over the past several years. The choice of ships and cruising styles have grown along with Alaska's popularity. Seven-day cruises sail along the protected waters of the Inside Passage with stops in colorful frontier towns such as Juneau, Skagway, and Sitka. Ships are always in sight of snow-capped peaks and the spectacular glacier formations of Glacier Bay. The Alaska cruise season is short: cruises sail from mid-May to early October and range from one to two weeks in length.

One-week cruises embark from northern ports such as Vancouver, Canada. Longer cruises embark from West Coast ports such as San Francisco or Los Angeles.

Rail and motocoach tours that travel deep into the interior are available on many Alaskan cruises.

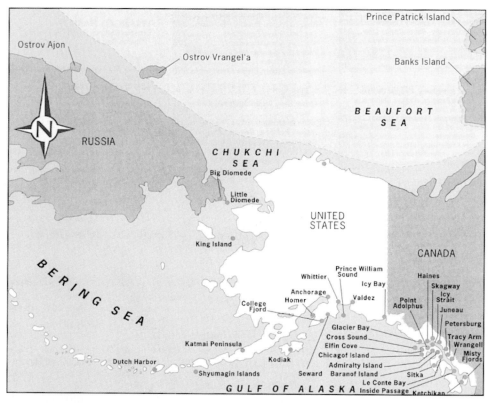

Figure 4.10 Alaska ports of call.

7-DAY CRUISE ON CRYSTAL CRUISES' *CRYSTAL HARMONY*

Day	Port	Arrive	Depart
Sunday	Vancouver		6:00 P.M.
Monday	Cruising Inside Passage		
Tuesday	Juneau	2:00 P.M.	12:00 midnight
Wednesday	Haines	8:00 A.M.	1:00 P.M.
	Skagway	2:00 P.M.	9:00 P.M.
Thursday	Cruising Glacier Bay		
Friday	Ketchikan (cruising Misty Fjord)	8:00 A.M.	1:00 P.M.
Saturday	Cruising Inside Passage		
Sunday	Vancouver	7:00 A.M.	

Cruise ship in Glacier Bay National Park, Alaska.

Hawaii

All Hawaiian cruises are operated by American Hawaii Cruises, which is owned and operated by a U.S. company. At the time of this publication, American Hawaii Cruises operates one ship, the SS *Independence*, which embarks from Honolulu on one-week cruises. This is an ideal way to get a taste of each island from the comfort of a cruise ship, with ports of call at the major islands of Maui and Kauai, and the big island of Hawaii. This is a port-intensive itinerary, with a new port visited each day. Hawaii cruises operate year-round.

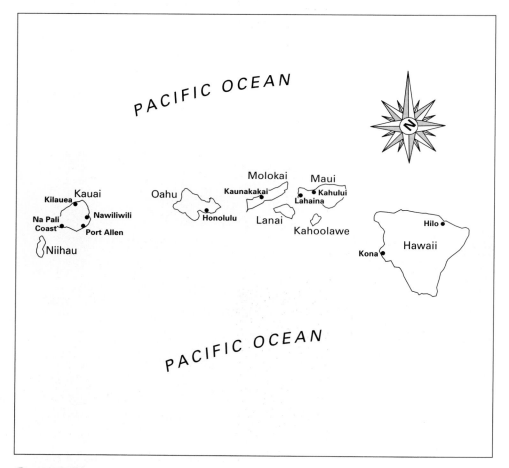

Figure 4.11

7-DAY CRUISE ON AMERICAN HAWAII CRUISES' SS *INDEPENDENCE*

Day	Port	Arrive	Depart
Saturday	Honolulu, Oahu		9:00 P.M.
Sunday	Kona, Hawaii	1:00 P.M.	
Monday	Kona, Hawaii		1:00 P.M.
Tuesday	Hilo, Hawaii	8:00 A.M.	7:00 P.M.
Wednesday	Kahului, Maui	8:00 A.M.	
Thursday	Kahului, Maui		6:00 P.M.
Friday	Nawiliwili, Kauai	8:00 A.M.	7:00 P.M.
Saturday	Honolulu, Oahu	7:00 A.M.	

Passenger ship *Yorktown Clipper* doing some whale watching during a recent cruise. Courtesy of Clipper Cruise Line.

Inland U.S. Rivers

The Mississippi and its tributaries offer hundreds of miles of cruise waters from the Gulf of Mexico up into America's heartland. The Delta Queen Steamboat Company operates authentic steam-powered paddle-wheelers

Figure 4.12 Inland U.S. rivers ports of call.

on leisurely trips from three to ten days in length. These year-round cruises extend north to Minneapolis–St. Paul during the warm summer months and concentrate in the southern areas during the winter and early spring.

7-DAY CRUISE ON DELTA QUEEN STEAMBOAT'S
AMERICAN QUEEN

Day	Port	Arrive	Depart
Saturday	New Orleans		7:00 P.M.
Sunday	Oak Valley, Louisiana	9:00 A.M.	7:00 P.M.
Monday	St. Francisville, Louisiana	9:00 A.M.	7:00 P.M.
Tuesday	Natchez, Mississippi	9:00 A.M.	7:00 P.M.
Wednesday	Vicksburg, Mississippi	9:00 A.M.	7:00 P.M.
Thursday	Steamboatin'		
Friday	Helena, Arkansas	9:00 A.M.	7:00 P.M.
Saturday	Memphis, Tennessee	9:00 A.M.	

Naturalist on board giving a lecture during a cruise to Alaska.

Europe (Mediterranean)

The Mediterranean offers many unique cruise experiences, from posh sophisticated beach resorts along the French Riviera to the ancient mysteries in the deserts of Egypt. This vast area is marketed as two general segments—Eastern and Western Mediterranean cruises. Some of the more lengthy itineraries may include ports of call from both areas. The principal season for Mediterranean cruises is during the summer months.

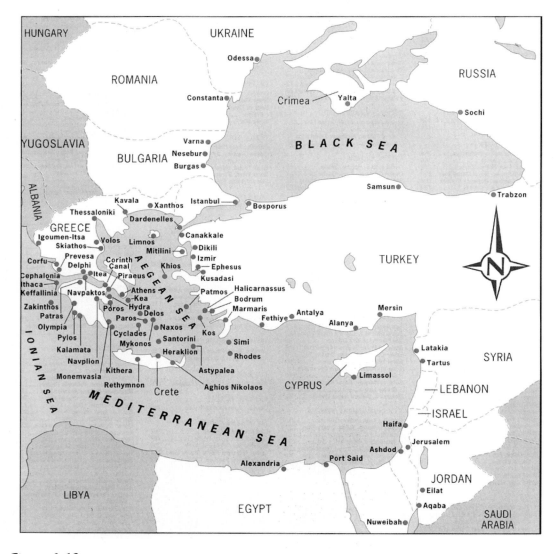

Figure 4.13

a. Southern Caribbean
b. Mexican Riviera
c. Eastern Caribbean
d. Panama Canal
e. Western Caribbean

9. Your clients are looking for fewer days at sea and more ports of call on their next seven-day cruise. Which of the following would you recommend?

a. Bermuda
b. Southern Caribbean
c. Eastern Caribbean
d. Western Caribbean
e. Mexican Riviera

10. Coastal China and Japan cruises can be taken in either direction: northbound or southbound. Which two ports of call serve as the embarkation/debarkation points?

a. Sydney, Australia, and Hong Kong
b. Hong Kong and Bangkok, Thailand
c. Sydney, Australia, and Singapore
d. Osaka, Japan, and Hong Kong
e. Ho Chi Minh City, Vietnam, and Singapore

11. Name three major cruise areas in the United States:

_____   _____   _____

12. Name three major cruise areas in Europe:

_____   _____   _____

13. Name three major cruise areas in the Pacific Rim:

_____   _____   _____

14. Your clients are repeat cruisers and are now looking for something more adventurous or unique in their next cruise. They can leave at any time and would like to go to South America. What three cruise itineraries would you suggest?

_____   _____   _____

15. What is the busiest cruise port in the world? _____

16. From which port do Southern Caribbean cruises usually depart?

_____

17. What company operates frequent riverboat cruises up and down the Mississippi River and its tributaries? _____

18. What company operates seven-day cruises in the Hawaiian Islands?

_____

19. Which cruise area in North America offers cruises along with optional land tours by either rail or motorcoach deep into the interior?

_____

True or False?

20. _____ The most popular cruise destination in the world is the West Indies.

21. _____ Eastern Caribbean cruises stop frequently in such ports as Bogotá, Colombia, and Caracas, Venezuela.

22. _____ The country of Panama is a frequent port of call on Panama Canal cruises.

23. _____ The only year-round cruise area in South America is the Galápagos Islands.

24. _____ Copenhagen is the primary embarkation port for Scandinavian cruises.

25. _____ A repositioning cruise is a good idea for most first-time cruise travelers.

26. _____ Barges and chartered yachts are popular ways to cruise the inland waterways of Great Britain and continental Europe.

27. _____ Extended cruises from Australia or New Zealand often include stops in exotic South Pacific islands such as Fiji and Tahiti.

28. _____ The islands of Bali and Jakarta, Indonesia, are visited often during cruises to the East Indies.

29. _____ Most cruises in Southeast Asia that visit ports in Vietnam, Thailand, and Malaysia are ten days or less in length.

30. _____ Beijing is a popular one-day stopover during coastal China cruises.

Resources and References 5

After completing Chapter 5, students will be able to:

- Describe the major sections, and interpret and access information from each of the following three major cruise reference guides:

  Official Steamship Guide International

  The *Official Cruise Guide*

  The CLIA *Manual*

- Interpret and access information from cruise brochures.

KEY TERMS

CLIA

CLIA *Manual*

Official Cruise Guide

Official Steamship Guide International

INTRODUCTION

The travel professional has a wealth of printed resources on hand to assist in the selling and booking of cruise travel. The four most often used resources are *Official Steamship Guide International*, the *Official Cruise Guide*, the CLIA *Manual*, and cruise brochures.

Each of the four major resources is presented in this chapter. In the following pages, full-page and cutaway samples from each resource are reprinted along with brief explanations of their content and format. Checkpoint exercises follow each section to help you learn how to use these resources effectively in the workplace.

OFFICIAL STEAMSHIP GUIDE INTERNATIONAL

This softcover publication is issued four times per year on a seasonal basis, in winter, spring, summer, and fall editions. Travel agencies subscribe to this resource, which costs approximately $90 for an annual subscription.

Figure 5.1 *Official Steamship Guide International.*

Official Steamship Guide International should be used as a general directory of cruise ships: what ships are traveling where and when. It won't provide detailed deck plans and rates, but it provides you with enough information to direct you to the specific cruise line and ships that you are trying to find.

The guide can be divided into six sections. Each section is described here with sample pages. Read the descriptions of each section, study the sample pages, and complete the Checkpoint exercises.

Contents

Figure 5.2 is the table of contents of a recent *Official Steamship Guide International*. At a glance, you can see the six major sections and page number references.

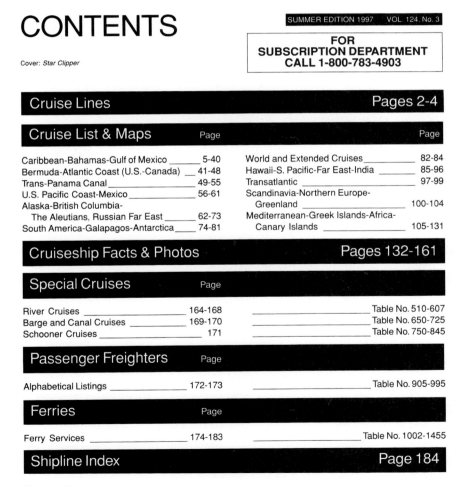

CONTENTS

Cover: *Star Clipper*

SUMMER EDITION 1997   VOL. 124, No. 3

FOR SUBSCRIPTION DEPARTMENT CALL 1-800-783-4903

Figure 5.2 Table of Contents, *Official Steamship Guide International.*

Section 1: Cruise Lines   This section provides an alphabetical list of cruise line companies with headquarters addresses and telephone and fax numbers for reservations.

Section 2: Cruise List & Maps   This section provides a chronological list of departure dates, cruise ships by name, embarkation point, length of cruise, ports of call, and minimum cabin rates by cruise area. There are also maps of the major cruise areas that locate and identify embarkation ports and major ports of call within each cruise region. This is a handy reference to find out which ship is traveling where, when, and for how long.

Section 3: Cruiseship Facts & Photos   This section provides an alphabetical list of cruise ships by name with statistical data, including passenger capacity, GRT, and photos of each ship.

Section 4: Special Cruises   This section provides data on which ships are operating any special or unique cruise itineraries.

Section 5: Passenger Freighters   This section provides a list, in table format, of freighters that operate cargo/passenger service to worldwide ports.

Section 6: Ferries   This section provides schedules of passenger/car ferry service between worldwide ports.

Shipline Index   This last section in the resource provides an alphabetical list of cruise ships by name and the page reference.

Checkpoint 5.1 _____

This exercise is designed to reinforce the major information sections of *Official Steamship Guide International*. Refer to Figure 5.2, a sample table of contents page, and indicate the page number(s) where you would find the answers to the following questions.

1. What ships operate cruises up and down the Mississippi River? _____

2. How frequently do passenger ferry services operate between Hyannis and Martha's Vineyard? _____

3. What does Carnival's megaship *Destiny* look like? _____

4. Where are some of the major ports of call on your client's next Alaskan cruise? _____

5. Does passenger freighter service operate between the West Coast of the United States and the Caribbean? _____

6. What ships are sailing to Bermuda next summer? _____

7. What is the space ratio (GRT divided by passenger capacity) of the *Splendour of the Seas*? _____

8. What number would you call to make cruise reservations on Princess Cruises for your client? _____

Cruise Lines

This section is the telephone directory for cruise line companies. For each cruise line represented, it lists the address of company headquarters, toll-free reservation numbers, and fax numbers. Refer to Figure 5.3, a sample page from the "Cruise Lines" section.

Checkpoint 5.2 _____

Refer to Figure 5.3, a sample page from the "Cruise Lines" section, and answer the following questions.

1. What number would you call to make reservations for your clients with Seabourn Cruise Line if your office is located in Chicago?

   _____

2. You are booking a group of more than 100 Kiwanis Club members with Princess Cruises next winter. What number would you call to make the

   group reservation if your office is located in Dallas? _____

3. You are planning a sales presentation to a local civic group regarding a Mediterranean cruise on Renaissance Cruises. You want to order brochures, posters, and a slide show or video to use during your sales presentation. What number would you call to request these sales

   materials? _____

4. You want to write a thank-you letter on behalf of your clients, who just had a wonderful cruise with Society Expeditions. You wish to address the letter to the company's chief executive officer. What is the address

   of this company's headquarters? _____

   _____

5. You have a group reserved on the *Radisson Diamond*, a ship operated by Radisson Seven Seas Cruises. They need a passenger name list from you

   today. What is their fax number? _____

 **CRUISE LINES**

260
PREMIER CRUISE LINES—400 Challenger Rd., Cape Canaveral, FL 32920, Tel: US (800) 327-7113; Group: US (800) 327-9703; FAX (407) 784-0954
3 and 4-night cruises from Port Canaveral— *Star/Ship Oceanic.*7-night—Walt Disney World package available (including either 3 or 4 night cruise). Call for rates.

265
PRINCESS CRUISES—10100 Santa Monica Blvd., Los Angeles, CA 90067, Tel: (800) 421-0522; (310) 553-1770; Sales (800) 527-6200; Group (800) 421-1700; FAX (310) 284-2844
Caribbean, Mexico, Trans-Panama Canal, Alaska, S. America, Canada—New England, Hawaii—Far East, Mediterranean, Scandinavia and Transatlantic—*Pacific Princess, Island Princess, Royal Princess, Sky Princess, Golden Princess, Star Princess, Crown Princess, Regal Princess, Sun Princess,* and *Dawn Princess.*

267
RADISSON SEVEN SEAS CRUISES—600 Corporate Dr., Ste. 410, Fort Lauderdale, FL 33334, Tel: (800) 285-1835; FAX (402) 431-5599
Caribbean, Mediterranean, Scandinavia, S. America, Antarctica, Alaska, Far East, and South Pacific—*Radisson Diamond, Song of Flower, Hanseatic, Bremen,* and *Paul Gauguin.*

268
REGAL CRUISES—4199 34th St. South, Ste. B103, St. Petersburg, FL 33711, Tel: (800) 270-SAIL; (813) 867-1300; FAX: (813) 867-1046
4, 5, and 6-night cruises to the Caribbean aboard the *Regal Empress.*

275
RENAISSANCE CRUISES, INC.—1800 Eller Drive, Suite 300, P.O. Box 350307, Fort Lauderdale, FL 33335-0307, Tel: (954) 463-0982; Reservations: (800) 525-5350; Sales: (800) 525-2450; FAX (954) 463-8125.
Far East, Mediterranean, Scandinavia, Africa, and Caribbean—*Renaissance V-VIII* and *Aegean I.*

280
ROYAL CARIBBEAN CRUISE LINE—1050 Caribbean Way, Miami, FL 33132, Tel: (800) 327-6700; FL (800) 432-6559; Dade County (305) 379-4731; Group (800) 327-2055; FL Group (800) 432-3568; Canada (800) 245-7225.
Caribbean, Bermuda, Trans Panama Canal, U.S. Pacific Coast, Alaska, Mediterranean and Scandinavian cruises—*Monarch of the Seas, Nordic Empress, Viking Serenade, Sovereign of the Seas, Sun Viking, Song of America, Majesty of the Seas, Legend of the Seas, Splendour of the Seas, Grandeur of the Seas, Enchantment of the Seas,* and *Rhapsody of the Seas.*

303
SEAWIND CRUISE LINE—1750 Coral Way, Miami, FL 33145, Tel: (800) 258-8006; (305) 573-7447; FAX (305) 285-9599
7-night Caribbean cruises from Aruba year round—*Seawind Crown.*

304
SEABOURN CRUISE LINE—55 Francisco St., San Francisco, CA 94133, Tel: (800) 929-9595; (415) 397-9595; CANADA, (800) 527-0999; TLX 205838 SEBRN UR; FAX (415) 391-8518
Caribbean, South America, Panama Canal, New England/Canada, Transatlantic, Mediterranean and Scandinavia—*Seabourn Pride, Seabourn Spirit,* and *Seabourn Legend.*

305
SEAESCAPE LIMITED—140 S. Federal Hwy., Dania, FL 33004, Tel: (800) 327-2005; Exec. Offices: (954) 925-9700
Daily cruises from Fort Lauderdale to Freeport and Nowhere—*Ukraina.*

307
STAR CLIPPERS, INC.—4101 Salzedo Ave., Coral Gables, FL 33146, Tel: (800) 442-0551; (305) 442-0550; FAX (305) 442-1611
Caribbean, Transatlantic and Mediterranean cruises aboard the 360 foot *Barquentine* sailing ships *Star Flyer* and *Star Clipper.*

312
SILVERSEA CRUISES—110 E. Broward Blvd., Fort Lauderdale, FL 33301, Tel: (800) 722-6655; (954) 522-2288; FAX (305) 522-4499.
Caribbean, S. America, Panama Canal, Mediterranean, Scandinavia, New England/Canada, Far East—*Silver Cloud* and *Silver Wind.*

313
SOCIETY EXPEDITIONS—2001 Western Ave., Ste. 300, Seattle, WA 98121, Tel: (800) 548-8669; (206) 728-9400; FAX (206) 728-2301.
Antarctica, Alaska and South Pacific cruises—*World Discoverer.*

314
STC SCANTRAVEL CENTER—66 Edgewood Avenue, Larchmont, NY 10538, Tel: (800) 759-7226; (914) 834-3944: FAX (914) 834-7528
Scandinavia, North Cape and Arctic cruises—*Funchal.*

345
SPECIAL EXPEDITIONS—720 Fifth Ave., New York, N.Y. 10019, Tel: (800) 762-0003; (212) 765-7740; FAX (212) 265-3770
Caribbean, Panama Canal, S. America—*Polaris.* U.S. Pacific Coast, Alaska—*Sea Bird* and *Sea Lion.* Caribbean and Mediterranean—*Sea Cloud.*

350
SUN LINE ROYAL OLYMPIC CRUISES—1 Rockefeller Plaza, Suite 315, NY, NY 10020, Tel: US (800) 872-6400; (212) 397-6400; CAN (800) 368-3888; FAX (212) 765-9685; TLX 236480 or 213735
Mediterranean, Scandinavia, Caribbean, South America, and Transatlantic cruises—*Stella Solaris, Stella Oceanis* and *Odysseus.*

363
TEMPTRESS CRUISES—351 N.W. Lejeune Rd., Suite 600, Miami, FL 33126, Tel: (800) 336-8423; (305) 643-4040; FAX (305) 643-6438.
Three- and six-night cruises from Costa Rica aboard the *Temptress.*

395
WINDSTAR CRUISES—300 Elliot Avenue West, Seattle, WA 98119, Tel: (800) 258-SAIL; Sales: (800) 544-0443; Exec. Offices: (206) 281-3535; FAX (206) 286-3229.
Caribbean, Transatlantic and Mediterranean—*Wind Star* and *Wind Spirit.* French Polynesian cruises—*Wind Song.*

400
WORLD EXPLORER CRUISES—555 Montgomery St., San Francisco, CA 94111-2544, Tel: (800) 854-3835; FAX (415) 391-1145
Fourteen-day educational and cultural Alaska Cruises May through August—*Universe Explorer.*

410
YACHTSHIP CRUISE LINE—520 Pike St., Ste. 1610, Seattle, WA 98101, Tel: (206) 623-2417; (800) 451-5952; (415) 393-1565; FAX (206) 623-7809
Pacific, Northwest and Alaska cruises—*Executive Explorer* and the *Wilderness Explorer.*

Figure 5.3 **Sample page from the "Cruise Lines" section.**

Cruise List & Maps

The "Cruise List & Maps" section is the largest one in this resource. It is divided into several major cruise areas such as the Caribbean, Bermuda, U.S. Pacific Coast and Mexico, Alaska, the South Pacific, the Far East, and the Mediterranean. Within each cruise area section, a list of cruise ships appears, in order by departure date. Below is a sample listing from the Caribbean section for Carnival Cruise Lines' *Sensation*, departing December 1. Figure 5.4 is a full sample page from this section.

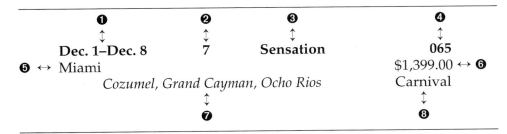

Explanation

❶ Embarkation and debarkation dates
❷ Number of nights
❸ Ship name
❹ Table number reference (refers to the listing in the "Cruise Lines" section)

❺ Port of embarkation
❻ Minimum cabin rate based on double occupancy
❼ Port-to-port itinerary
❽ Cruise line name

Checkpoint 5.3 _____

Refer to Figure 5.4, a sample page from the Caribbean–Bahamas–Gulf of Mexico cruise list section, and answer the following questions.

1. The *Mercury* operates a Western Caribbean cruise that embarks on March 15.

   a. How many nights is this cruise? _____

   b. What is the port of embarkation? _____

   c. What cruise line operates the *Mercury*? _____

   d. What is the U.S. port of call on this itinerary? _____

   e. What are the ports of call in the Caribbean and Mexico?

   _____

   f. What day does this cruise return? _____

   g. What is the minimum rate per person, based on double occupancy?

   $ _____

CARIBBEAN • BAHAMAS • GULF OF MEXICO

Leave	Return	No. of Nights	Ship	Table No. Min. Rate Operator
Mar. 14-Mar. 21 Fort Lauderdale		7	Century	068 $849.00
San Juan, St. Thomas, St. Maarten, Nassau				Celebrity
Mar. 14-Mar. 21 San Juan		7	Dawn Princess	265 $1,299.00
Barbados, St. Lucia, Martinique, St. Maarten, St. Thomas				Princess
Mar. 14-Mar. 21 San Juan		7	Fascination	265 $1,309.00
St. Thomas, St. Maarten, Dominica, Barbados, Martinique				Carnival
Mar. 14-Mar. 21 San Juan		7	Galaxy	068 $899.00
Catalina Island, Barbados, Martinique, Antigua, St. Thomas				Celebrity
Mar. 14-Mar. 21 Miami		7	Grandeur of the Seas	280 $1,699.00
Labadee, San Juan, St. Thomas, Coco Cay				Royal Caribbean
Mar. 14-Mar. 21 Miami		7	Imagination	065 $1,309.00
Playa del Carmen, Cozumel, Grand Cayman, Ocho Rios				Carnival
Mar. 14-Mar. 21 Tampa		7	Noordam	190 $1,298.00
Grand Cayman, Santo Tomas de Castilla, Playa del Carmen, Cozumel				Holland America
Mar. 14-Mar. 21 San Juan		7	Rhapsody of the Seas	280 $1,699.00
Oranjestad, Willemstad, Philipsburg, St. Thomas				Royal Caribbean
Mar. 14-Mar. 21 Barbados		7	Sea Goddess I	115 $4,600.00
St. Lucia, Bequia, Grenada, Isla de Margarita, Tobago, Mayreau				Cunard
Mar. 14-Mar. 21 Miami		7	Sensation	065 $1,309.00
San Juan, St. Thomas, St. Maarten				Carnival
Mar. 14-Mar. 21 Fort Lauderdale		7	Sun Princess	265 $1,299.00
Princess Cays, Ocho Rios, Grand Cayman, Cozumel				Princess
Mar. 14-Mar. 21 Fort Lauderdale		7	Westerdam	190 $1,248.00
Nassau, San Juan, St. John, St. Thomas, Half Moon Cay				Holland America
Mar. 14-Mar. 24 Fort Lauderdale		10	Ryndam	190 $2,278.00
Nassau, St. Thomas, St. Maarten, St. Lucia, Barbados, Half Moon Cay				Holland America
Mar. 15-Mar. 22 Miami		7	Carnival Destiny	065 $1,609.00
San Juan, St. Croix, St. Thomas				Carnival
Mar. 15-Mar. 22 Tampa		7	Celebration	065 $1,309.00
Grand Cayman, Playa del Carmen, Cozumel, New Orleans				Carnival
Mar. 15-Mar. 22 Fort Lauderdale		7	Costa Romantica	090 $899.00
Key West, Cozumel, Ocho Rios, Grand Cayman				Costa
Mar. 15-Mar. 22 Fort Lauderdale		7	Costa Victoria	090 $899.00
San Juan, St. Thomas/St. John, Serena Cay, Nassau				Costa
Mar. 15-Mar. 22 Miami		7	Enchantment of the Sea	280 $749.00
Key West, Playa del Carmen, Cozumel, Ocho Rios, Georgetown				Royal Caribbean
Mar. 15-Mar. 22 San Juan		7	Inspiration	065 $1,309.00
St. Thomas, Guadeloupe, Grenada, St. Lucia, Santo Domingo				Carnival
Mar. 15-Mar. 22 Santo Domingo		7	Island Breeze	130 $895.00
Barbados, St. Lucia, Guadeloupe, St. Maarten, St. Thomas				Dolphin
Mar. 15-Mar. 22 Miami		7	Majesty of the Seas	280 $1,599.00
Labadee, Ocho Rios, Georgetown, Playa del Carmen, Cozumel				Royal Caribbean
Mar. 15-Mar. 22 Fort Lauderdale		7	Mercury	068 $899.00
Key West, Cozumel, Montego Bay, Grand Cayman				Celebrity
Mar. 15-Mar. 22 San Juan		7	Monarch of the Seas	280 $1,699.00
St. Thomas, Fort-de-France, Bridgetown, St. John's, Philipsburg				Royal Caribbean
Mar. 15-Mar. 22 Montego Bay		7	Ocean Breeze	130 $995.00
Cartagena, Panama Canal/Gatun Lake, San Blas Islands, Puerto Limon				Dolphin
Mar. 15-Mar. 22 Miami		7	Sea Breeze	130 $645.00
Playa del Carmen/Cozumel, Montego Bay, Grand Cayman				Dolphin
Mar. 15-Mar. 22 Fort Lauderdale		7	Veendam	190 $1,488.00
St. Kitts, St. John, St. Thomas, Half Moon Cay				Holland America
Mar. 16-Mar. 27 San Juan		11	Tropicale	065 $1,689.00
St. Thomas, St. Barts, St. Lucia, Aruba, Panama Canal/Gatun Lake, Ocho Rios				Carnival
Mar. 17-Mar. 27 Galveston		10	Stella Solaris	350 $2,740.00
Cozumel, Playa del Carmen, Isla de Roatan, Santo Tomas de Castilla, Puerto Cortes, Belize City				Sun Line
Mar. 18-Mar. 28 Miami		10	Splendour of the Seas	280 $2,399.00
Playa del Carmen, Cozumel, Georgetown, Ocho Rios, St. Thomas, San Juan, Labadee				Royal Caribbean
Mar. 19-Mar. 29 Fort Lauderdale		10	Crown Princess	$2,678.00
Cartagena, Panama Canal/Gatun Lake, Limon, San Blas Islands, Cozumel				Princess
Mar. 20-Mar. 27 New Orleans		7	Celebration	065 $1,309.00
Tampa, Grand Cayman, Playa del Carmen, Cozumel				Carnival
Mar. 20-Mar. 30 Fort Lauderdale		10	Horizon	068 $1,149.00
St. Maarten, St. Lucia, Barbados, Antigua, St. Thomas				Celebrity
Mar. 21-Mar. 28 Fort Lauderdale		7	Century	068 $899.00
Ocho Rios, Grand Cayman, Cozumel, Key West				Celebrity
Mar. 21-Mar. 28 San Juan		7	Dawn Princess	265 $1,299.00
Aruba, Caracas, Grenada, Dominica, St. Thomas				Princess
Mar. 21-Mar. 28 San Juan		7	Fascination	065 $1,309.00
St. Thomas, St. Maarten, Dominica, Barbados, Martinique				Carnival
Mar. 21-Mar. 28 San Juan		7	Galaxy	068 $899.00
Catalina Island, Barbados, Martinique, Antigua, St. Thomas				Celebrity
Mar. 21-Mar. 28 Miami		7	Grandeur of the Seas	280 $1,699.00
Labadee, San Juan, St. Thomas, Coco Cay				Royal Caribbean
Mar. 21-Mar. 28 Miami		7	Imagination	065 $1,309.00
Playa del Carmen, Cozumel, Grand Cayman, Ocho Rios				Carnival

Figure 5.4 **Sample page from the "Cruise List & Maps" section.**

2. Name the ships that operate one-week cruises from San Juan during March: _____

3. Your clients want a seven-day cruise from either Miami or Fort Lauderdale departing March 21. This is their first cruise and they would like to visit St. Thomas (for shopping) and Puerto Rico (for sightseeing).

   a. What ship would you suggest? _____

   b. What company operates this ship? _____

   c. What is the embarkation port? _____

   d. In addition to St. Thomas and San Juan, what other ports does this ship visit? _____

   e. What is the minimum cabin rate per person on this ship (double occupancy)? $ _____

4. Your clients, who are repeat cruisers, are now looking for a ten- or eleven-day cruise to the Southern Caribbean. They can leave any time during March and prefer either Celebrity Cruises or Holland America Line. What ships would you suggest and from which port does each embark? _____

Cruiseship Facts & Photos

This section provides exactly what the name implies: an alphabetical list of cruise ships by name along with their vital statistics such as vessel tonnage, when the ship was built or refurbished, passenger capacity, number of cabins, and a list of passenger facilities and services on board. A photo of each ship is also included. This section is helpful as a quick reference for individual ships. Figure 5.5 is a sample page from the "Cruiseship Facts & Photos" section.

Checkpoint 5.4 _____

Refer to Figure 5.5, a sample page from the "Cruiseship Facts & Photos" section and answer the following questions.

1. Which cruise line operates the *Costa Victoria*? _____

2. In which country is the *Crown Princess* registered? _____

3. Of the cruise ships featured, which is the largest in terms of gross registered tonnage? _____

 # Cruiseship Facts and Photos

Costa Victoria
Costa Cruises
Registry: Liberia

Tonnage: 75,000
Built: Due June 1996
Refurbished:
Former Name(s):
Crew Nationality: Italian, International
Languages Spoken: N/A
No. of Staff: N/A
Passenger Capacity: 1,950
No. of Cabins: 964
Length: 824 ft. **Width:** 105.5 ft.

Cruising Speed: 23 knots
Facilities: Observation lounge, atriums, Alfresco cafe, spa, fitness and beauty center, dining rooms, casino, disco, show lounge, library, bars/lounges, children/teens rooms

A/C: Yes   **Stabilizers:** Yes

Crown Majesty
Majesty Cruise Line
Registry: Bahamas

Tonnage: 20,000
Built: 1993
Refurbished:
Former Name(s): Cunard Dynasty*
Crew Nationality: Officers: N. European & Scandinavian, Filipino
Languages Spoken: English, Filipino, etc.
No. of Staff: 300
Passenger Capacity: 820

No. of Cabins: 410
Length: 537 ft.   **Width:** 74 ft.
Cruising Speed: 18.5 knots
Facilities: One outdoor pool, 3 whirlpools, wading pool, beauty salon & massage, fitness spa, duty-free shop & boutique, photo shop, air conditioning, Crowncierge Service

A/C: Yes   **Stabilizers:** Yes

Crown Princess
Princess Cruises
Registry: Italy

Tonnage: 70,000
Built: 1990
Refurbished:
Former Name(s):
Crew Nationality: Italian, Portuguese & British
Languages Spoken: English, Italian, Portuguese
No. of Staff: 678
Passenger Capacity: 1,596
No. of Cabins: 792
Length: 804 ft.   **Width:** 105 ft.

Cruising Speed: 19.5 knots
Facilities: Observation lounge, nightclub, casino, pizzeria, speciality bar, youth center, pool, library, card room, showroom, wine bar, shopping arcade, buffet restaurant, lounge, cinema, patisserie, fitness, beauty center, discotheque

A/C: Yes   **Stabilizers:** Yes

Crystal Harmony
Crystal Cruises
Registry: Bahamas

Tonnage: 49,400
Built: 1989
Refurbished:
Former Name(s):
Crew Nationality: Norwegian, Japanese, International & European
Languages Spoken: English, Spanish, Portuguese, Italian, German, Norwegian, French, Japanese
No. of Staff: 475

Passenger Capacity: 960
No. of Cabins: 480
Length: 791 ft.   **Width:** 97 ft.
Cruising Speed: 22 knots
Facilities: Crystal dining room, 2 dining restaurants, spa, fitness center, shopping, casino, golf simulator, theatre, indoor/outdoor pool, pool with swim-up bar, galaxy show lounge

A/C: Yes   **Stabilizers:** Yes

Crystal Symphony
N.Y.K./Crystal Cruises
Registry: Bahamas

Tonnage: 50,000
Built: May 1995
Refurbished:
Former Name(s):
Crew Nationality: Norwegian, Japanese, International
Languages Spoken: English
No. of Staff: 530
Passenger Capacity: 960
No. of Cabins: 480
Length: 778 ft.   **Width:** 98 ft.

Cruising Speed: 22 knots
Facilities: Dining Room, 2 restaurants, theatre, library/business center, casino, shopping area, lounges, galaxy showroom, spa, 2 swimming pools, handicapped facilities

A/C: Yes   **Stabilizers:** Yes

Dawn Princess
Princess Cruises
Registry: Italy

Tonnage: 77,000
Built: 1996
Refurbished:
Former Name(s):
Crew Nationality: American, International
Languages Spoken: English, International
No. of Staff: 900
Passenger Capacity: 1,950
No. of Cabins: 1,011

Length: 856 ft.   **Width:** 106 ft.
Cruising Speed: 19 knots
Facilities: Two atriums, 2 showrooms, indoor/outdoor food court, casino, shopping promenade, health & fitness center, library, pizzeria, golf center, teen & youth centers, wine bar, observation lounge

A/C: Yes   **Stabilizers:** Yes

Figure 5.5 Sample page from the "Cruiseship Facts & Photos" section.

4. How many cabins are there on the *Crystal Harmony*?

_____

5. Calculate the passenger space ratio for:

   a. *Dawn Princess*   _____

   b. *Crystal Harmony*   _____

   c. *Crown Majesty*   _____

6. List the ships from question 5 in order from the most spacious to the least spacious in terms of space ratio.

   (1) _____   (2) _____   (3) _____

7. Of the ships featured, which is the longest? _____

8. Which ships offer children's/teen rooms and facilities? _____

_____

Special Cruises

This section includes special or unique voyages such as river cruises, barge and canal trips through inland waterways, schooner cruises, and passenger freighters. This section doesn't provide a lot of detailed information, but is a quick reference for when special cruises are scheduled, where they are going, and for how long.

For example, suppose your clients want to take a deluxe canal cruise through the inland waterways in France. This section will list the cruise lines that operate this type of experience. Or, your clients may be asking about the Windjammer Barefoot cruises where they can participate in the sailing of the ship. This section will inform you of the seasonal schedules, reservation numbers, and descriptions of some of the vessels.

Figure 5.6 shows two sample pages from the "Special Cruises" section.

Checkpoint 5.5 _____

Refer to Figure 5.6, two sample pages from the "Special Cruises" section, and answer the following questions.

1. Your client wants to take a cruise on the Amazon River in South America.

   a. What cruise company operates this type of cruise?

   _____

RIVER CRUISES

UNITED STATES AND CANADA

510
THE DELTA QUEEN STEAMBOAT CO.—1380 Port of New Orleans Place, New Orleans, LA, 70130-1890, Tel: (800) 543-1949; TLX 5101007509; FAX: (504) 585-0630

Delta Queen
11 NIGHTS New Orleans to St. Louis

12 NIGHTS Pittsburgh to New Orleans

8 NIGHTS Cincinnati (Round Trip)

8 NIGHTS Little Rock to Cincinnati

7 NIGHTS New Orleans (Round Trip); New Orleans to Galveston; New Orleans to Memphis; Memphis to Cincinnati; Chattanooga to Nashville; St. Louis to St. Paul; St. Paul to St. Louis; Cincinnati to St. Louis; Nashville to Little Rock

6 NIGHTS New Orleans (Round Trip); Memphis to New Orleans; St. Louis to Nashville; Galveston to New Orleans; New Orleans to Galveston; St. Louis to Ottawa; Ottawa to St. Louis

5 NIGHTS New Orleans (Round Trip); Cincinnati to Pittsburgh

4 NIGHTS New Orleans (Round Trip); Cincinnati (Round Trip); Memphis to St. Louis

3 NIGHTS New Orleans (Round Trip)

ALL SAILINGS ARE YEAR ROUND   RATES: $390.00 to $7,420.00

Mississippi Queen
11 NIGHTS New Orleans to St. Louis

7 NIGHTS New Orleans (Round Trip); New Orleans to Memphis; St. Louis to St. Paul; St. Paul to St. Louis; Memphis to Chattanooga; Memphis to Cincinnati

6 NIGHTS New Orleans (Round Trip); Memphis to New Orleans; St. Louis to Nashville; St. Louis to Cincinnati; Nashville to Cincinnati; Memphis to Nashville

5 NIGHTS New Orleans (Round Trip); Cincinnati to Pittsburgh

4 NIGHTS New Orleans (Round Trip); Pittsburgh to Cincinnati

3 NIGHTS New Orleans (Round Trip); St. Louis (Round Trip); Pittsburgh (Round Trip)

2 NIGHTS New Orleans (Round Trip)

ALL SAILINGS ARE YEAR ROUND   RATES: $390.00 to $6,790.00

American Queen
14 NIGHTS St. Paul to New Orleans

7 NIGHTS New Orleans (Round Trip); New Orleans to Memphis; Memphis to New Orleans; St. Louis to St. Paul; St. Paul to St. Louis; Cincinnati to Memphis

6 NIGHTS New Orleans (Round Trip); New Orleans to Memphis; Memphis to New Orleans; St. Louis to Louisville; St. Paul to St. Louis; St. Louis to Cincinnati

5 NIGHTS New Orleans (Round Trip); Memphis to St. Louis; Cincinnati to Memphis

4 NIGHTS New Orleans (Round Trip); Memphis to St. Louis; St. Louis to Louisville; Louisville to St. Louis; St. Louis (Round Trip)

3 NIGHTS New Orleans (Round Trip); Cincinnati (Round Trip); St. Paul (Round Trip) Memphis (Round Trip)

SAILINGS ARE YEAR ROUND   RATES: $390.00 to $8,660.00

515
AMERICAN WEST STEAMBOAT CO.—Two Union Square, 601 Union Street, #4343, Seattle, WA 98101, Tel: Reservations (800) 434-1232, Administration (206) 292-9606, Fax: (206) 340-0975

Queen of the West
7 NIGHTS Portland, Hood River/Maryhill, Snake River, Lewiston, Pendelton, Longview/Mt. St. Helens, Astoria, Portland
Sailing Dates: 1997: Every Saturday from May 10-Dec. 27.   From $945.00

525
ST. LAWRENCE CRUISE LINES—253 Ontario St., Kingston, Ontario, Canada K7L 2Z4, Tel: (613) 549-8091; Res: US & CANADA (800) 267-7868

Canadian Empress
4 NIGHTS Kingston, 1000 Islands Retreat, Brockville, Upper Canada Village, Coteau Landing, Montreal (terminates)

4 NIGHTS Montreal, Cote Ste. Catherines, Upper Canada Village, Brockville, Rockport, Kingston (terminates)

6 NIGHTS Kingston, 1000 Islands Retreat, Upper Canada Village, Coteau Landing, Montreal, Trois Rivieres, Quebec City (terminates)

6 NIGHTS Quebec City, Trois Rivieres, Montreal, Upper Canada Village, Brockville, Rockport, Kingston (terminates)

5 NIGHTS Kingston, 1000 Islands Retreat, Upper Canada Village, Coteau Landing, Montreal, Montebello, Ottawa (terminates)

5 NIGHTS Montebello, OKA, Montreal, Upper Canada Village, Rockport or Brockville, Kingston (terminates)

SOUTH AMERICA

530
AMAZON TOURS & CRUISES—8700 W. Flagler St., Suite 190, Miami, FL 33174, Tel: (800) 423-2791; (305) 227-2266; FAX (305) 227-1880

M/V Rio Amazonas
6 NIGHTS Iquitos, Pevas, Ampiyacu River, Bora and Huitoto Villages, Pevas, Shishita & Cochaquinas Rivers, Chimbote, Ataquari River, Lake Caballacocha, Leticia (Colombia), Tabatinga (Brazil), San Pablo, Mayaruna River, Pijuyal, Iquitos
Sailing Dates: Every Sunday $950.00-$1,105.00

3 NIGHTS Iquitos, Pevas, Ampiyacu River, Bora and Huitoto Villages, Pevas, Shishita River, Chimbote, Ataquari River, Lake Caballacocha, Puerto Alegria, Leticia (Colombia), Tabatinga, (Brazil), (terminates)
Sailing Dates: Every Sunday $525.00-$580.00

M/V Arca and M/V Amazon Explorer
6 NIGHTS Iquitos, Pevas, Bora & Huitoto Indian villages, Shishita, Cochaquinas River, Chimbote, Ataquari River, Caballo Cocha, Leticia/Tabatinga shore excursion, Puerto Alegria, San Pablo, Mayarunas River, Pevas, Pijuyal, Ampiyacu River, Iquitos
Sailing Dates: Sundays $850.00

3 NIGHTS Iquitos, Pevas, Bora & Huitoto Indian villages, Shishita, Cochaquinas River, Chimbote, Ataquari River, Caballo Cocha, Leticia/Tabatinga
Sailing Dates: Sundays $495.00

M/V Delfin and Amazon Discoverer
6 NIGHTS Iquitos, Tamshiyacu, Tahuayo, Yanayacu River area, Nauta, Maranon and Ucayali Rivers, Yarapa, Nauta Cano, Iquitos
Sailing Dates: Selected Sundays $695.00

3 NIGHTS Iquitos, Tamshiyacu, Tahuayu, Maranon & Ucayali Rivers, Nauta Cano, Yarapa River, Iquitos
Sailing Dates: Selected Sundays $375.00

EUROPE—AFRICA—FAR EAST

535
ESPLANADE TOURS—581 Boylston Street, Boston, MA 02116, Tel: (800) 426-5492; FAX (617) 262-9829

NILE RIVER
M/S Regency
14 DAY LAND/CRUISE (7 Day Cruise) Cairo, Luxor, Edfu, Kom-Ombo, Aswan, Kom-Ombo, Esna, Luxor, Dendera, Abydos, Luxor, Cairo
Sailing Dates: Year Round

RUSSIAN RIVERS
M/V Kirov
11 & 12 DAY CRUISES St. Petersburg/Moscow—11 Nights; Moscow/St. Petersburg—12 Nights Lake Ladoga, Svir River, Lake Onega, Voga-Baltic Canal. Extensive sightseeing in Moscow and St. Petersburg and sites along the way.
Sailing Dates: May through October

EUROPEAN RIVERS
Crown Blue Line
1 & 2 week itineraries in France, Holland and Great Britain. Self-drive, April through October

540
EUROCRUISES—303 W. 13th St., New York, NY 10014, Tel: (800) 688-3876; (212) 691-2099; FAX: (212) 366-4747. Brochures 1-800-661-1119

Blue Danube I & II
7 NIGHTS Budapest-Berching, Budapest, Vienna, Durnstein, Melk, Passau, Regensburg, Kelheim, Berching
Sailing dates: July 6-13; Aug. 3-8, Aug. 9-16; Aug. 17-24; Aug. 31-Sept. 7; Sept. 14-21   From $1,550.00-$2,770.00

7 NIGHTS Berching-Budapest, Berching, Kelheim, Regensburg, Passau, Melk, Durnstein, Vienna, Budapest
Sailing dates: July 5-12; July 13-20; July 27-Aug. 3; Aug. 10-17; Aug. 16-23; Aug. 24-31; Sept. 7-14; Sept. 21-28   From $1,550.00-$2,770.00

12 NIGHTS Budapest, Vienna, Melk, Grein, Passau, Regensburg, Kelheim, Hilpotstein, Nuremberg, Bamberg, Hassefurt, Volkach, Kitzingen, Würburg, Miltenberg, Aschaffenburg, Rüdesheim, Düsseldorf
Departure dates: Sept. 28-Oct. 10   From $2,635.00-$4,709.00

14 NIGHTS Budapest, Esztergom, Vienna, Melk, Grein, Passau, Regensburg, Kelheim, Hilpoltstein, Nuremberg, Bamberg, Hassfurt, Volkach, Kitzingen, Würburg, Miltenberg, Aschaffenburg, Rüdesheim, Cologne, Amsterdam
Departure dates: Sept. 14-20   From $1,550.00-$2,770.00

Figure 5.6 Two sample pages from "Special Cruises" section.

 # BARGE and CANAL CRUISES

650
ABERCROMBIE & KENT—1520 Kensington Road, Oak Brook, IL 60521-2141, Tel: (800) 323-7308; (630) 954-2944; Fax: (630) 954-3324; TLX 210126

3- to 6-night cruises in France, England, Holland, Belgium, Germany and Austria. Tuesday, Wednesday, Saturday and Sunday departures in France, Sunday and Wednesday departures in England, Sunday and Wednesday departures in Holland/Belgium. Seine, Yonne, Rhone Rivers, Burgundy Canal; Saone, Burgundy, Provence, Loire Valley, Franche Comté, Champagne and Central France. Biking, hot air ballooning, wine, opera and gourmet cruises and family cruising (in France) available. Rates from $1160 (France). River Thames Windsor to Oxford in England. Rates from $1090 (England). Amsterdam, Gouda, Rotterdam, Delft, Den Haag, Alkmaar, Purmerend in Holland and to Bruges in Belgium. Rates from $990 (Belgium) and $1390 (Holland/Belgium). Special Garden, Biking and Fine Arts departures (Holland/Belgium). The Danube from Passau to Vienna from $3,650; Holland on the Marjorie from $1,850.

655
THE BARGE COMPANY—44 Ambra Vale East, Bristol BS8 4RE. U.K. Tel: (117) 9299921; FAX (117) 9254712. International Toll Free: 1-800-367-0303

Independent brokerage service for all the luxury barges of France, UK, and Holland. Individual bookings and group charters on over 50 barges.

657
THE BARGE LADY: ELLEN SACK—101 West Grand Avenue, Suite 200, Chicago, Illinois 60610. Tel: (800) 880-0071; FAX (312) 245-0952

Send for our 1997 newsletter which describes 50 canal barges in France, Holland, England, Scotland, and Ireland. Specialists in golfing — barging in the Scottish Highlands, Holland at Tulip Time, and the largest selection of vessels in France, ranging from super deluxe to inexpensive and informal. Also, specialized cruises for wine connoisseurs. All vessels personally inspected. Commissions begin at 10%; overrides available for group bookings.

658
BORDEAUX CANAL CRUISING/THE JULIA HOYT—5 Ledgewood Way, Suite 6, Peabody, MA 01960, Tel. (800) 852-2625, (508) 535-5738, FAX (508) 535-5738

Exclusive Charter-Canal Cruise on Luxury 85 ft. Dutch Barge, *The Julia Hoyt*, in S.W. France on the Canal Lateral a la Garonne. Customized itineraries—1 week charters available May thru October—$3,280 per person based on 4 person occupancy.

659
B&V ASSOCIATES—140 East 56th ste 4C New York, NY 10022, Tel: 1-800-438-4748, Fax: 1-212-688-9467, Admin: 212-688-9538

6-night barge cruises in France/England/Belgium/Holland and River Boat Cruises in France, Germany, Holland, Austria and Hungary. Prices vary from $1,690 to $3,180 p/p. All our luxury cruises include: Accommodation with private bath, all meals, table wines, alcoholic beverages consumed aboard, all sightseeing and admittance fees as stipulated, use of bicycles and other facilities and roundtrip transfers from specified meeting point. Also: Add-on chateaux tours and apartment rentals in Europe; individuals and groups.

665
THE BARGE BROKER: Howard L. Dougherty—2124 Broadway, Boulder, CO 80302, Tel: (800) 275-9794; (303) 447-3582; FAX (303) 447-2487

Now representing a series of boats that offer 3 to 6 night cruises from 4 passengers up on the canals of France, England, Holland and Belgium. Call for information and brochures.

676
ETOILE DE CHAMPAGNE—88 Broad Street, Boston, MA 02110, Tel: (800) 280-1492; FAX (617) 426-4689

6 to 12 night luxury barge cruises in France, Belgium, Netherlands and introducing a new cruise on the Mosel River in Germany — April-October. Three decks with 7 deluxe oversized cabins, salon, dining room, lounge and two terraces. Cruise includes all meals, drinks, pickup in Paris, Amsterdam and Trier and daily tours. Individual bookings and charters available.

678
EURO CHARTERS DIVISION OF TRAVEL BY GINNY, INC.—417 Brevard Avenue, Cocoa, Florida 32922, Tel: (800) 950-5610 or (407) 632-5610; FAX (407) 632-5878

New in 1997 cruises on the *Nymphea* in the Loire Valley and the *Kir Royal* in the Seine and Oise Valleys. Plus *Le Bon Vivant, Joie de Vivre, Belle Epoque, L'Impressionniste, Le Papillon, Penelope, Reine Pedauque, Niagara, Stella, La Vancelle, Sherborne, Athos, Avenir, Rosa, Lafayette, Escargot, Litote, Libellule,* and *Anacoluthe* on the canals of France. In England the *Actief* and in Ireland the *Bona Spes.* Spring time cruises in Holland. October and November cruises in Provence. And river cruises on the Rhone, Saone, Rhine, Moselle, Danube and Elbe.

679
EXCLUSIVETOURS—Suite 1504, 60 Bloor St. West, Toronto, Ont. M4W 3B8 in Canada 1-800-269-0969; FAX (416) 925-8887, Tel: (416) 925-2889

Le Bon Vivant, La Joie de Vivre, La Belle Époque, L'Impressioniste, La Reine Pedauque, Niagara, Nymphea, Stella, Anjodi, Rosa, Actief, Bona Spes, Vertrouwen, Anacoluthe, Chanterelle, Escargot, Abercrombie, Lafayette, Litote, Libellule, La Vancelle, Penelope, Sherborne, Athos, Avenir. 6 night luxury hotel barge cruises on the rivers and canals of France, England, Ireland, Scotland and Holland. From approximately Canadian $400 per night.

680
EUROPEAN WATERWAYS—140 East 56th Street, Suite 4C, New York, NY 10022, Tel: (800) 217-4447, (212) 688-9489; FAX (800) 296-4554, (212) 688-3778

Barge owners and representatives since 1974 luxury canal and river cruises aboard company owned and represented vessels in France — Burgundy, upper Loire, Midi, Provence, Alsace, Gascogny, Beaujolais, Loire Valley, Paris Region, England — River Thames, Holland — Tuliptime, Scotland — Loch Ness and the Great Glen, Eire — River Shannon and Belgium.

Vessels include: *Anjodi, La Belle Époque, Stella, La Vancelle, Joie de Vivre, Rosa, Actief, Bona Spes, L'Impressionniste, Bon Vivant, Kir Royal, La Reine Pedauque, Niagara, Nymphea,* River Cruises in Germany. Theme Cruise Calendar: Winetasting, tennis, golf, antiques and auctions, culinary summits and markets and more.

Cruises feature: Gourmet cuisine, private baths, regional wines, open bar, daily escorted sightseeing, bicycles, roundtrip transfers from specified meeting point and attention to detail! Rates: $1,690-$3,400 p/p 6 nights. Also: Add-on chateaux tours and apartment rentals in Europe, individuals and groups.

685
FRENCH COUNTRY WATERWAYS, LTD.—P.O. Box 2195; Duxbury, MA 02331, Tel: (800) 222-1236; MA (617) 934-2454; FAX (617) 934-9048

Six-night canal cruises in France aboard the luxury hotel Barges, *Esprit, Horizon II, Liberte,* and *Nenuphar.* Itineraries include wine cruises in Burgundy aboard the 18 passenger *Esprit* and the 12 passenger *Horizon II,* historic Burgundy cruises aboard the 12 passenger *Nenuphar,* and gourmet cruises in Burgundy on the 8 passenger *Liberte.* Cruises feature air-conditioned staterooms or suites with private baths, gourmet cuisine, regional wines, and open bar, 3-star restaurant dinner ashore. Rates start at $2795 per person and include all meals, wines, use of bicycles, daily escorted sightseeing, and transfers to and from major cities. Optional hot air ballooning on all vessels. Charter rates. Non-smoking.

690
GOTA CANAL—Bergen Line, Inc., 405 Park Avenue, New York, NY 10022, Tel: (800) 323-7436; (212) 319-1300; FAX (212) 319-1390. Also Euro Cruises, 303 West 13th St., New York, NY 10014, Tel: (800) 688-3876; (212) 691-2099; FAX 366-4747

4-day and 6-day trips on the Gota Canal from Stockholm to Gothenburg and reverse, May to September. Stops include Soderkoping, Berg, Motala, Vadstena, and Trollhattan. Rates from $775, food incl., 2-3 departures a week.

705
INLAND VOYAGES—23 Adlington Road, Bollington, Macclesfield, Cheshire, SK105JT England, Tel. and Fax 01625-576880, U.S. Representative: McGregor Travel Management, 112 Prospect Street, Stamford, Conn. 06901, Tel: 203-978-5010, 800-786-5311, Fax: 203-978-5027

Six-night cruise on the *Luciole* hotel barge on the waterways of Burgundy, France, include gourmet food and wine, escorted transfers Paris/Dijon. Individual bookings and charters available.

Figure 5.6 (continued)

b. This cruise company offers three- or six-night Amazon cruises. What is the port of embarkation for all departures?

_____

c. On what day of the week do the six-night cruises depart?

_____

d. Name the vessel that operates three-night Amazon cruises *every* Sunday. _____

e. What is the minimum rate per person, based on double occupancy, on the six-night cruise on the M/V *Arca*? $_____

2. Name the ship that operates a two-week Mississippi River cruise from St. Paul to New Orleans. _____

3. The company called Eurocruises operates river cruises through Europe during the summer months.

a What are the names of Eurocruises' two ships?

_____

b. What is the port of embarkation for the two-week departure on September 20? _____

c. At what city does this river cruise terminate?

_____

4. A very popular and unique vacation experience is to take a leisurely cruise by barge through the canals of Europe. French Country Waterways, Ltd., is only one of many companies that operates barge and canal cruises.

a. Where is this company located?_____

b. If your agency is located in the Boston area, what number would you call for more information? _____

c. How long are these cruises? _____

d. Which of their vessels operates a gourmet cruise through Burgundy, France? _____

e. What is the minimum rate per person on these cruises? $_____

f. List all features and services that are included in the cost of these cruises: _____

5. Abercrombie & Kent is also an established and well-known operator of European canal cruises and land tours.

   a. This company offers golf, antiques, and _____ tours in England.

   b. The Rhine River cruises in Germany start at $ _____ per person.

   c. In addition to gourmet and wine cruises, hot-air ballooning is available in the country of _____. Prices for cruises in this country start at $_____ per person.

Ferry Services

This section provides a listing of worldwide passenger ferry services. For each passenger ferry company listed, the following data are provided: ports, duration of trip, season of operation, cost for adult passengers, and whether cars are accepted. Figure 5.7 is a sample page from the "Ferries" section.

Checkpoint 5.6 _____

Refer to Figure 5.7, a sample page from the "Ferries" section, and answer the following questions.

1. The Golden Gate Ferry Service operates between San Francisco and Sausalito.

   a. How long does the trip take? _____

   b. What is the price per adult? $_____

   c. Are cars accepted? _____

2. During what two months of the year is ferry service to and from Fire Island not provided? _____

3. Your client wants some information about the ferry service between Vancouver and Victoria in British Columbia, Canada.

   a. What company operates ferry service between these two cities?

   _____

   b. How long does the trip take each way? _____

   c. How many daily departures are there during off season? _____

   d. What is the approximate price per adult? $_____

   e. Are cars allowed? _____. If yes, what is the approximate cost for a car? $_____

FERRY SERVICES
United States — Canada — Alaska

Ports	Trip Duration	Season	Off Season	Adults	Cars

ALASKA STATE FERRY SYSTEM—(Alaska Marine Highway)—Box 25535, Juneau, AK 99802-5535, Tel: (800) 642-0066, (907) 465-3441 U.S./Canada

Ports	Trip Duration	Season			
Bellingham-Ketchikan	36 hrs	12/mo			
Prince-Skagway	2 days	12/mo			
Bellingham-Skagway	3 days	12/mo			
Hyder-Ketchikan	10 hrs	4/mo			

Also stops in Metlakatla, Hollis, Wrangell, Petersburg, Kake, Angoon, Sitka, Hoonah, Tenakee, Juneau, Pelican and Haines.

Seward-Kodiak	13½ hrs	9/mo			
Kodiak-Homer	9½ hrs	9/mo			
Whittier-Valdez	7 hrs	5/mo			

Also stops in Cordova, Port Lions, Seldovia, Chignik, Sand Point, King Cove, Cold Bay, Akutan, False Pass and Dutch Harbor (Unalaska), Tatitick, Chenega Bay.

BAY STATE CRUISE COMPANY, INC.—67 Long Wharf, Boston, MA 02110. Tel: 617-723-7800; FAX 617-457-1425. Contact: Pamela J. Burns.

Boston Harbor & Islands	90 mins.	May-Oct.	Call	$7.50/$5.50	No
Inner Harbor & Waterfront	55 min.	May-Oct.	Call	$5/$3	No
Provincetown, Cape Cod	3 hrs.	May-Oct.	N/A	$29/$20	No
	ea. way				

BC FERRIES (or British Columbia Ferry Corporation)—1112 Fort Street, Victoria, British Columbia V8V 4V2, Canada. Tel: Victoria (604) 669-1211

Vancouver/Victoria (Tsawwassen/Swartz Bay)	1½ hrs	16/day	8+/day	$6.50	$27.00
Vancouver/Nanaimo (Horseshoe Bay/Nanaimo)	1½ hrs	12/day	8/day	$6.50	$27.00
Vancouver/Nanaimo (Tsawwassen/Nanaimo)	2 hrs	8/day	8/day	$6.25	$27.00 above are weekend rates (weekday rates lower)
Vancouver/S. Gulf Is.	varies	varies	varies	$7.75	$33.50
Vancouver Is./S. Gulf Is.	varies	varies	varies	varies	varies
Vancouver Is./N. Gulf Is.	varies	varies	varies	varies	varies
Prince Rupert/ Queen Charlotte Is.	8 hrs	4/wk	3/wk	$22.25	$84.75 peak prices
Prince Rupert/Port Hardy	15 hrs	June-Sept. 3-4/wk	Oct./May 1/wk	$100.00	$206.00 peak season prices

(Schedules and fares subject to change without notice.)

BEAVER ISLAND BOAT CO.—102 Bridge St., Charlevoix, MI 49720, Tel: (616) 547-2311

Charlevoix-St. James	2¼ hrs	July-Aug. 2-3/day	Apr.-Dec. 1/day	$17.00 1-way $29 r.t.	$49.00 1-way $98 r.t.

BELL ISLAND FERRY SERVICE—P.O. Box 1510, St. John's, Newfoundland, Canada. Tel: 709-895-3541

Bell Island and Portugal Cove Newfoundland	20 min.	12 mos.		$0.50 Can. Return Fare	$3.00 Can. Return Fare

2 vessel operation, mid May to January 1.
1 vessel operation, January to mid May.

BLACK BALL TRANSPORT, INC.—Port Angeles Terminal, 101 E. Railroad Ave., Port Angeles, WA 98362, Tel: (360) 457-4491; Fax: (360) 457-4493; Victoria Terminal, 430 Belleville St., Victoria, British Columbia V8V 1W9, Canada, Tel: (250) 386-2202, Fax: (250) 386-2207; Main Office: 10777 Main St., Ste. 106, Bellevue, WA 98004, Tel: (206) 622-2222, Fax: (206) 622-2225.

Port Angeles-Victoria	1 hr 35 min	all year operation: mid-May-mid-Oct. 4/day mid-Oct.-Dec., March-mid-May 2/day Jan.-mid-March* 1/day		$6.50	$27

*Usually out of service for up to 15-day period, late January to early February for annual re-fit/overhaul.

BLUE WATER FERRY LTD.—St. Clair Pkwy., Sombra, Ont., Canada. N0P 2H0. Tel: (519) 892-3879

Sombra, Ont.- Marine City, Mich.	5 min.	all year operation	Jan.-Mar.	$.50 U.S. or Can.	$4.00 per car regardless of number of passengers

2 ferries operating daily May-Oct; each capacity 12 autos

BRIDGEPORT & PORT JEFFERSON STEAMBOAT CO.—102 W. Broadway, Port Jefferson, L.I., NY 11777, Tel: (516) 473-0286; (203) 367-3043

Bridgeport-Port Jefferson	1¼ hrs	Call for info			

CAPE ISLAND EXPRESS LINES, INC.—P.O. Box 4095, New Bedford, MA 02741, Tel: (617) 997-1688

New Bedford-Vineyard Haven		May-Oct. 3-4/day		$16.00 rt	

CAPE MAY-LEWES FERRY—1-800-64 FERRY; Reservations: (800) 717 SAIL, Lewes Terminal, Lewes, DE 19958, Tel: (302) 644-6030; Cape May Terminal, N. Cape May, NJ 08204, Tel: (302) 644-6030; Lewes Terminal

Cape May-Lewes				$4.50/$3	$18

CASCO BAY LINES—Commercial & Franklin Sts., P.O. Box 4656 D.T.S., Portland, ME 04112, Tel: (207) 774-7871; FAX: (207) 774-7875
Year-round commuter, charter and cruise services.

CATALINA PASSENGER SERVICE—400 Main St., Balboa Pavilion, Balboa, CA 92661, Tel: (714) 673-5245

Avalon, Catalina Island	75 min	Mar.-Nov.		$33.00	Roundtrip

CIRCLE LINE—Pier 83, West End of 42nd St., New York, NY 10036, Tel: (212) 563-3200

New York City A.	3 hrs	Leaves at 10:30 and 2:00 daily	$18.00		
Cruise around Manhattan	2 hrs				

CLARKE TRANSPORT CANADA INC.—199 rue Maynard, C.P. 172, La Traverse Riviere-du-Loup, St. Simeon Ltee, Riviere-du-Loup, Quebec, Canada G5R 3Y8, Tel: (418) 862-9545

Riviere-du-Loup-St. Simeon	1 hr	Apr.-Dec.			

CLIPPER NAVIGATION, INC.—2701 Alaskan Way (Pier 69), Seattle, WA 98121, Tel: (206) 448-5000; Victoria (250) 382-8100

Seattle-Victoria	from 2 hrs	Year round Daily departures		$69-$104 rt	

COASTAL TRANSPORT LTD.—165 Union St., Ste. 402, Saint John, N.B. E2L, 5C7, Canada. Tel: (506) 636-3922

Black's Harbor-North Head	1½ hrs	3/day	3/day	$8.40	$25.20

CROSS SOUND FERRY SERVICES, INC.—Box 33, New London, CT 06320, Tel: (203) 443-5281

New London-Orient Point	1½ hrs	16/day	4/day	$8.50	Mon-Sun $29.00

C.T.M.A.—Souris, Prince Edward Island, C0A 2B0, Canada, Tel: (902) 687-2181

Souris-Iles de la Madeline	5 hrs	daily		$33.00	$63.00

Now you have to make reservations at phone no. (418) 986-3278 for the months of June 15, July, Aug. up to Sept. 15. There is no boat from January 28th to April 1st every year.

CUTTYHUNK BOAT LINES, INC.—Pier 3-Fisherman's Wharf, New Bedford, MA 02740, Tel: (508) 992-1432

New Bedford-Cuttyhunk	1 hr	Fri., Sat., 2 times a week Sun., Mon. 2 trips daily Tues.-Thurs. 1 trip daily		$10.75 one-way $15.75 day trip	No

FIRE ISLAND FERRIES, INC.—99 Maple Ave., P.O. Box 311-P, Bay Shore, New York 11706, Tel: (516) 665-3600 or 666-3600

Ocean Beach, Fire Island	30 min.	Mar.-Dec.	Jan.-Feb.	$5.75	no cars
Seaview, Fire Island	30 min.	Mar.-Oct.	Nov.-Feb.	$5.75	
Saltaire, Fire Island	30 min.	Mar.-Dec.	Jan.-Feb.	$5.75	no cars
Kismet, Fire Island	30 min.	Mar.-Oct.	Nov.-Feb.	$5.75	
Fair Harbor, Fire Island	30 min.	Mar.-Dec.	Jan.-Feb.	$5.75	no cars
Dunewood, Fire Island	30 min.	Mar.-Oct.	Nov.-Feb.	$5.75	
Ocean Bay Park, Fire Island	30 min.	Mar.-Oct.	Nov.-Feb.	$5.75	no cars

No passenger service provided in January and February

FORT GATES FERRY—Gateway Fishing Corp., Star Route #1, Box 350, Crescent City, FL 32112, Tel: (904) 467-2411.

Eastside of St. Johns River to West Side	10 min	All year		$8.00 AM/car	

GOLDEN GATE FERRY SERVICE—101 East Sir Francis Drake Blvd., Larkspur, California 94939-1899. Tel: (415) 332-6600.

Larkspur-San Francisco	45 mins.	All year		$2.50/ $4.25*	Passenger Ferry
Sausalito-San Francisco	30 mins.	All year		$4.25	Passenger Ferry

*$2.50 one way adult fare weekdays, $4.25 weekends/holidays. Family fare on weekends and holidays, children age 5 and under ride free when accompanied by a full fare paying adult on Larkspur and Sausalito ferries (Limit 2 per adult).

Figure 5.7 Sample page from the "Ferries" section.

This softcover resource book is printed annually by *Travel Weekly*, a major travel trade publication. Travel agents can subscribe to this resource for approximately $95 per year. Unlike *Official Steamship Guide International,* which is more of a quick, at-a-glance directory, the *Official Cruise Guide* provides a lot more detailed information and pictures. This guide is considered the primary cruise resource because of the amount of data that it provides.

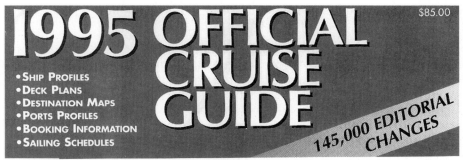

Figure 5.8 *Official Cruise Guide.*

R

Radisson Seven Seas Cruises	800-333-3333
Regal Cruise Line	800-270-SAIL
Regency Cruises	800-REGENCY
Renaissance Cruises	800-525-2450
Robert River Rides	800-457-9975
Royal Caribbean International	800-327-6700
Royal Cruise Line	800-227-4534

Figure 5.9 **Cruise lines' reservation numbers.**

CELEBRITY CRUISES CLIA

Century	86
Horizon	88
Meridian	90
Zenith	92
Booking information	24

Figure 5.10 **Alphabetical list of cruise lines.**

The intention of this publication is to create a one-stop source that provides answers to all questions regarding the matching of cruise to client, booking a cruise, and ship particulars. With this in mind, the *Official Cruise Guide* is a compendium of information essential to booking a cruise. The resource is so vast (well over 750 pages of information) that we will list the 18 general sections of this resource with brief descriptions. Cutaway examples of many of these sections will be provided as illustrations.

Cruise Lines' Reservation Numbers   An alphabetical listing of cruise lines, with toll-free reservation numbers (Figure 5.9).

QUICK CHECK!

What number would you call to make reservations on Royal Caribbean International's *Destiny*? _____

Alphabetical List of Cruise Lines   A listing of all the lines included in the guide, along with the names of the ships they operate (Figure 5.10).

QUICK CHECK!

Name the four ships that Celebrity Cruises operates:

_____   _____   _____   _____

Travel Agent's Booking Information   Details the booking/reservation policies and procedures of more than 140 cruise lines and provides answers to many of the most frequently asked booking-related questions (Figure 5.11).

NORWEGIAN CRUISE LINE

2 Alhambra Plaza, Coral Gables, FL 33134
Phone: 305-447-9660 Fax: 305-443-2464
Reservations: 800-327-7030

Ships Operated: Dreamward, Norway, Seaward, Southward, Starward, Westward, Windward

Sales Office: Brook House, 229-243 Shepherds Bush Rd., Hammersmith, London, W6 7NL England   Phone: 71-493-6041 Fax: 81-748-4542

Sales Office: Hoffsveien 15, PO Box 224, Skoyen, Oslo 2, 0212 Norway   Phone: 472732955 Fax: 472732975

Sales Office: Ecrit, 11 Bis Avenue de Madrid, F-9220 Neuilly, Paris, France   Phone: 1-4530-1866 Fax: 1-4250-1878

Sales Office: Pfingstweidstr. 4, D-60316 Frankfurt-am-Main 1, Germany   Phone: 69-490161 Fax: 69-440007

Methods of Payment: American Express, MasterCard, Visa, Agency Check, Personal Check, Traveler's Check

Deposits: $100-$200 due within 1 week of booking

Final Payment: 45 days prior to departure

Levels of Commission: 10% on cruise and air/sea package

Group Bookings: 16 people minimum

Insurance: Baggage and personal effects

Single Rate: 50–100% above double rate

Double Occupancy cabins offered on a Share Basis: Guaranteed at rate chosen

Cancellation Policy: Cancellations 35 days prior to departure result in a $100 cancellation fee; 29 days prior, $200 fee; within 4 days of departure, no refund

Figure 5.11 **Travel agent's booking information.**

QUICK CHECK!

1. Name the seven ships that Norwegian Cruise Line operates:

   _____   _____   _____

   _____   _____   _____

   _____

2. You have two clients booked on Norwegian Cruise Line's *Norway.* What is the minimum required amount of deposit for a party of two? $_____

3. Your clients (a party of two) are booked on the *Dreamward,* sailing June 30. If they cancel on June 2 (four weeks before departure), what is the cancellation penalty? $_____

4. What is the level of commission for travel agencies? _____

Figure 5.12 **Alphabetical index of ships.**

Alphabetical Index of Ships   A listing of ship names along with the cruise lines with which they are associated (Figure 5.12).

QUICK CHECK!

1. Name the cruise line that operates each of the following ships:

   Queen Elizabeth II _____

   Queen of Sheba _____

Former Names Index   Ships have a habit of switching owners and names over the years. This index arranges the ships alphabetically by their original or former names, followed by their present names (Figure 5.13).

Former Names	Present Names
F	
Fair Majesty	**Star Princess**
Fairland	**Fair Princess**
Fairsea	**Fair Princess**
Fairsky	**Sky Princess**
Fairwind	**Dawn Princess**
Festival	**Silja Festival**
FiestaMarina	**Olympic**
Finnstar	**The Pearl**
Flandre	**Pallas Athena**
Flotel Francisco	**Flotel Orellana**
Flying Cloud	**Fantome**
France	**Norway**
Frederico "C"	**SeaBreeze**
Free State Mariner	**Monterey**
Frontier Spirit	**Bremen**

Figure 5.13 **Former names index.**

QUICK CHECK!

1. Your clients are sailing on the *Norway.* They know that this ship has changed ownership and once sailed under another name. What was the former name of the *Norway?* ______________________
2. The ship that was called *Fairwind* is now operating under a new name. What is it? ______________________

Length of Cruise Index A reference organized by the length (in days) of each itinerary for every ship listed in the guide (Figure 5.14).

QUICK CHECK!

Your clients are looking for a fourteen-day cruise. Name three ships that operate this length of cruise:

______________ ______________ ______________

7 Day Cruises

CostaAllegra *CS*..........85
CostaClassica *CS*..........85
CostaRiviera *CS*..........96
CostaRomantica *CS*..........96
Crown Odyssey *CS*..........236
Crown Princess *CS*..........170
Cunard Countess *CS*..........108
Cunard Crown Jewel *CS*..........113
Cunard Princess *CS*..........109

14 Day Cruises

Crown Odyssey *CS*..........236
Crystal Harmony *CS*..........98
Crystal Symphony *CS*..........99
Cunard Princess *CS*..........109
Delta Queen *RC*..........309
Explorer *DE*..........261
Island Princess *CS*..........176

Figure 5.14 **Length of cruise index.**

	1995		1990
	Year Refurbished		Year Refurbished
American Queen		Aranui II	
Century		Bremen	
Crystal Symphony		CostaMarina	
Erasmus		**Crown Princess** 1992	
Legend of the Seas		**Crystal Harmony**	
Oriana			
Reef Endeavour			

Figure 5.15 Index of ships by date built and date refurbished.

Index of Ships by Date Built   A reference organized by date built that includes the date of last refurbishment (Figure 5.15).

QUICK CHECK!

Your clients are sailing on the *Legend of the Seas*. They want to sail on one of the newer ships. Is this a new ship (built during the last ten years)? _____ In what year was it built? _____

Index of Ships by GRT   An overview of ships arranged in order of size (largest to smallest) as measured by gross registered tonnage and including passenger capacity (Figure 5.16).

QUICK CHECK!

1. Your clients feel more comfortable on a large ship. They are trying to choose between the *Majesty of the Seas* and the *Star Princess*. Which one would you suggest, based on tonnage? _____

2. Which ship has more elbow room (that is, which ship has a higher space ratio)—the *Star Princess* or the larger ship *Norway*? _____

Index of Ships by Passenger Capacity   An overview of ships arranged by passenger capacity, from highest to lowest, and including gross registered tonnage (Figure 5.17).

SHIP	GROSS REGISTERED TONNAGE (GRT)	PASS. CAP.
Norway	76,049	2022
Majesty of the Seas	73,941	2744
Monarch of the Seas	73,941	2772
Sovereign of the Seas	73,192	2276
Fantasy	70,367	2634
Ecstasy	70,367	2594
Sensation	70,367	2594
Fascination	70,367	2594
Crown Princess	70,000	1590
Regal Princess	70,000	1590
Legend of the Seas	70,000	1808
Century	70,000	1740

69,999–60,000

SHIP	GROSS REGISTERED TONNAGE (GRT)	PASS. CAP.
Queen Elizabeth II	67,139	1850
Oriana	67,000	1975
Star Princess	63,500	1490

Figure 5.16 Index of ships by GRT.

1,299–1,200

SHIP	PASSENGER CAPACITY	GRT
Statendam	1266	55,451
Maasdam	1266	55,451
Ryndam	1266	55,451
Windward	1246	41,000
Dreamward	1242	41,000
Star of Texas	1240	27,250
Noordam	1214	33,930
Nieuw Amsterdam	1214	33,930
Sky Princess	1200	46,000
Royal Princess	1200	45,000

1,199–1,100

SHIP	PASSENGER CAPACITY	GRT
EugenioCosta	1158	30,000
Song of Norway	1155	23,005
Nordic Prince	1144	23,149
Rotterdam	1114	38,645
Meridian	1106	30,440

Figure 5.17 Index of ships by passenger capacity.

QUICK CHECK!

1. Which ship carries more passengers, the *Sky Princess* or the *Ryndam?*

   _____

2. Which ship is under 28,800 GRT but has a capacity of over 1,200 passengers? _____ What is this ship's space ratio? _____

Theme Cruise Index A listing of the types and availability by departure date of theme and/or special-interest cruises and the ships on which they are offered (Figure 5.18).

Theme Cruises

Listed below is a selection of special-interest or theme cruises offered by the various cruise lines. The "themes" run the gamut from fantasy and escapist to cultural and enrichment.

Refer to individual sailing schedules on page 654 for itemized itineraries.

EUROPEAN WATERWAYS

Antiques & Auctions	Actief	River Thames, England	April, Oct
Art & Architecture	Anjodi	Provence, France	April, Nov
	La Belle Epoque	Provence, France	Oct–Dec
Culinary Summit	La Belle Epoque	Burgundy, France	May–Oct
Golf Charters	Anjodi	Provence, France	March, Nov

NORWEGIAN CRUISE LINE

Big Band Cruise	Norway	Miami, FL	Nov 25
Comedy Cruise	Norway	Miami, FL	June 10
Country Music Cruise	Norway	Miami, FL	Jan 14, April 22
Fitness & Beauty Cruise	Norway	Miami, FL	Oct 21
50's & 60's Theme	Norway	Miami, FL	September 30

Figure 5.18 Theme cruise index.

QUICK CHECK!

1. Your clients are sailing on Norwegian Cruise Line's *Norway* on November 25. What's the theme of this cruise? _____

2. Your clients are looking for a European cruise that features culinary techniques. Which ship operated by European Waterways would you suggest? _____

   When does this ship operate this type of cruise? _____

Special Program Index   This section provides a rundown of ships offering special cruise programs such as honeymoon, male host, children's, and spa cruises (Figure 5.19).

CHILDREN'S PROGRAM	PAGE
Azerbaydzhan, *CTC Cruise Lines*	97
Britanis, *Fantasy Cruises*	135
Canberra, *P & O Cruises*	164
Celebration, *Carnival Cruise Lines*	71
Century, *Celebrity Cruises*	86
CostaAllegra, *Costa Cruise Lines*	85
CostaClassica, *Costa Cruise Lines*	85
CostaRiviera, *Costa Cruise Lines*	96
CostaRomantica, *Costa Cruise Lines*	96
Crown Odyssey, *Royal Cruise Line*	236
Crystal Harmony, *Crystal Cruises*	98
Cunard Crown Jewel, *Cunard Crown*	113
Daphne, *Costa Cruise Lines*	96
Dolphin IV, *Dolphin Cruise Line*	128

HONEYMOON PROGRAM	PAGE
Century, *Celebrity Cruises*	86
Club Med 1, *Club Med Cruises*	282
Club Med 2, *Club Med Cruises*	282
Constitution, *American Hawaii Cruises*	72
CostaAllegra, *Costa Cruise Lines*	85
CostaClassica, *Costa Cruise Lines*	85
CostaRomantica, *Costa Cruise Lines*	96
Crown Odyssey, *Royal Cruise Line*	236

HOST PROGRAM (FOR UNESCORTED WOMEN)	PAGE
Actief, *Abercrombie & Kent*	312
Century, *Celebrity Cruises*	86
Crown Odyssey, *Royal Cruise Line*	236
Crystal Harmony, *Crystal Cruises*	98

SPA PROGRAM	PAGE
Black Prince, *Fred Olsen Cruise Lines*	136
Celebration, *Carnival Cruise Line*	71
Century, *Celebrity Cruises*	86
Club Med 1, *Club Med Cruises*	282
Club Med 2, *Club Med Cruises*	282
Constitution, *American Hawaii Cruises*	72

Figure 5.19 **Special program index.**

QUICK CHECK!

1. You are booking a honeymoon couple on their first cruise. Name at least two ships operated by Costa Cruise Lines that offer special honeymoon deals: ____________________ ____________________

2. Your client, a single woman, is traveling by herself. She is interested in a ship that offers a male host program. Which of these ships would you suggest?

a. *Club Med 1* c. *Century*
b. *Constitution* d. *CostaRiviera*

3. Your clients are traveling with their two children (under age 15). They definitely want to book on a ship that offers planned activities and structured programs for children. Which two ships would you suggest?

a. *Club Med 2* c. *Celebration*
b. *Constitution* d. *Century*

EGYPT/NILE RIVER

ABU TIG, EGYPT
Nile Monarch, *Swan Hellenic Cruises* *332*

ABYDOS, EGYPT
Jasmin, *Wings Tours & Nile Cruises* *334*
Orchid, *Wings Tours & Nile Cruises* *334*
Sun Boat III, *Abercrombie & Kent* *303*

ASSIOUT EL BALYANA
Nile Monarch, *Swan Hellenic Cruises* *332*
Sun Boat II, *Abercrombie & Kent* *303*

ASWAN, EGYPT
Isis, *Hilton Intl Nile Cruises* *322*
Jasmin, *Wings Tours & Nile Cruises* *334*
Nephtis, *Hilton Intl Nile Cruises* *322*
Nile Monarch, *Swan Hellenic Cruises* *332*

Orchid, *Wings Tours & Nile Cruises* *334*
Osiris, *Hilton Intl Nile Cruises* *322*
Queen of Sheba, *Nabila Nile Cruises* *327*
Sun Boat II, *Abercrombie & Kent* *303*
Sun Boat III, *Abercrombie & Kent* *303*

BALLIANA, EGYPT
Nile Monarch, *Swan Hellenic Cruises* *332*

BENI HASAN, EGYPT
Nile Monarch, *Swan Hellenic Cruises* *332*

BENI SUEF, EGYPT
Nile Monarch, *Swan Hellenic Cruises* *332*
Sun Boat II, *Abercrombie & Kent* *303*

CAIRO, EGYPT
Island Princess, Princess Cruises **176**

Nile Monarch, *Swan Hellenic Cruises* *332*
Sun Boat II, *Abercrombie & Kent* *303*

EDFU, EGYPT
Isis, *Hilton Intl Nile Cruises* *322*
Jasmin, *Wings Tours & Nile Cruises* *334*
Nephtis, *Hilton Intl Nile Cruises* *322*
Nile Monarch, *Swan Hellenic Cruises* *332*
Orchid, *Wings Tours & Nile Cruises* *334*
Osiris, *Hilton Intl Nile Cruises* *322*
Queen of Sheba, *Nabila Nile Cruises* *327*
Sun Boat II, *Abercrombie & Kent* *303*
Sun Boat III, *Abercrombie & Kent* *303*

LUXOR, EGYPT
Isis, *Hilton Intl Nile Cruises* *322*
Island Princess, Princess Cruises **176**
Jasmin, *Wings Tours & Nile Cruises* *334*
Nephtis, *Hilton Intl Nile Cruises* *322*
Nile Monarch, *Swan Hellenic Cruises* *332*
Orchid, *Wings Tours & Nile Cruises* *334*
Osiris, *Hilton Intl Nile Cruises* *322*
Queen of Sheba, *Nabila Nile Cruises* *327*
Sun Boat II, *Abercrombie & Kent* *303*
Sun Boat III, *Abercrombie & Kent* *303*

Figure 5.20 Worldwide cruising areas and ports of call.

Worldwide Cruising Areas & Ports of Call This section presents multicolored, detailed maps of major cruise areas and ports of call throughout the world. In addition, it lists the ships that stop at each port. These maps are helpful aids when discussing different cruise itineraries with clients (Figure 5.20).

QUICK CHECK!

1. Your clients are interested in a Nile cruise. A popular five-day trip cruises between Luxor and Aswan. Name at least four cruise ships that stop at both of these popular Nile River ports.

   ____________________ ____________________

   ____________________ ____________________

2. Name three ships that include Cairo, Egypt, as a port of call.

   ______________ ______________ ______________

3. Is Abu Simbel a major port of call on most Nile cruises? ______________

Worldwide Index of Ports of Call A comprehensive alphabetical reference of all ports visited by the ships listed in the guide. Ports are divided into 23 geographic areas around the world, and each port can be found (with a roster of ships stopping there) on the page indicated (Figure 5.21).

O

Oahu, HI	*Hawaii*	393
Oak Alley, LA	*US & Canada/Inland Waterways*	399
Oakland, CA	*US & Canada/West Coast*	402
Oban, Scotland	*British Isles*	427
Ocho Rios, Jamaica	*Western Caribbean*	372
Ochoa Beach, Galapagos	*South America*	407
Odessa, Ukraine	*Eastern Mediterranean*	417
Oka, PQ	*US & Canada/Inland Waterways*	399
Okinawa, Japan	*Orient*	437
Olden, Norway	*Scandinavia & Northern Europe*	425
Olympia, Greece	*Eastern Mediterranean*	417
Oporto, Portugal	*Western Mediterranean*	412
Oranjestad, Aruba	*Southern Caribbean*	384
Orcas Island, WA	*US & Canada*	402
Orinoco River, Venezuela	*South America*	407
Osaka, Japan	*Orient*	437
Oslo, Norway	*Scandinavia and Europe*	425

Figure 5.21 **Worldwide index of ports of call.**

QUICK CHECK!

1. Ocho Rios, Jamaica, is a port of call on a Western Caribbean itinerary. You want to find a list of ships that stop there. What's the page number? _____

2. Olympia, Greece, is a port of call in what cruise area? _____
   On what page can you find a list of ships that stop there? _____

Cruise Reference by Port of Departure   An alphabetical arrangement of ports of departure and the ships which leave from them (Figure 5.22).

QUICK CHECK!

1. Your clients want to depart from San Juan on a southern Caribbean cruise. Which of the ships listed below DOES NOT depart from this port?
   a. *Horizon*   c. *Legend of the Seas*
   b. *Nieuw Amsterdam*   d. *Crystal Harmony*

2. Which ship operated by Royal Caribbean International departs from San Francisco? _____

SAN FRANCISCO, CALIFORNIA

Crystal Symphony, *Crystal Cruises* 99
Fair Princess, *Princess Cruises*...172
Legend of The Seas, *Royal Caribbean International* 206
Nieuw Amsterdam, *Holland America Line*...137
Royal Odyssey, *Royal Cruise Line* 242

SAN JUAN, PUERTO RICO

CostaClassica, *Costa Cruise Lines* 85
Crown Odyssey, *Royal Cruise Line*..236
Crystal Harmony, *Crystal Cruises*..98
Cunard Countess, *Cunard Crown* 108
Fascination, *Carnival Cruise Lines* 83
Festivale, *Carnival Cruise Lines*...83
Horizon, *Celebrity Cruises* 88
Legend of The Seas, *Royal Caribbean International* 206
Meridian, *Celebrity Cruises* 90
Monarch of The Seas, *Royal Caribbean International* 212
Pacific Princess, *Princess Cruises* 176

Figure 5.22 **Cruise reference by port of departure.**

Worldwide Cruise Reference by Date and Departure Port   A chronological arrangement of cruises organized by date of departure (within each of 23 cruising areas), followed by a rundown of the port of departure and the length of each cruise (Figure 5.23).

QUICK CHECK!

1. Your clients want to depart during the first week in September on a seven-day cruise to Alaska. They prefer Holland America Line and want to depart from Vancouver. Which ship(s) would you suggest? _____

2. Which ship offers a ten-day cruise to Alaska from Seattle, Washington?

_____

Sailing Schedules   This section contains a ship-by-ship rundown of the itineraries of each vessel listed in the guide, including date of departure, port of departure, length of cruise, ports of call, and rates (Figure 5.24).

ALASKA

SEPTEMBER 1, 1995

PORT OF DEPARTURE	SHIP/CRUISE LINE	LENGTH OF TRIP
Seward, Alaska	**Regent Star,** *Regency Cruises*	7 Days
Vancouver, British Columbia	**Regent Sea,** *Regency Cruises*	7 Days

SEPTEMBER 2, 1995

PORT OF DEPARTURE	SHIP/CRUISE LINE	LENGTH OF TRIP
Juneau, Alaska	**Spirit of Discovery,** *Alaska Sightseeing/Cruise West*	7 Days
Seattle, Washington	**Spirit of '98,** *Alaska Sightseeing/Cruise West*	10 Days
Seward, Alaska	**Regal Princess,** *Princess Cruises*	7 Days
Vancouver, British Columbia	**Crown Princess,** *Princess Cruises*	7 Days
	Nieuw Amsterdam, *Holland America Line*	7 Days
	Sky Princess, *Princess Cruises*	7 Days

Figure 5.23 Worldwide cruise reference by date and departure port.

RYNDAM, Holland America Line

DEPARTURE DATE	PORT OF DEPARTURE	LENGTH	PORTS OF CALL	FARE: PP DBL OCC
January 3, 13, 23, **February** 2, 12, 22, **March** 4, 14, 24, **April** 3, 13, **October** 21, 31, **November** 10, 20, 30 **December** 10, 1995	Ft Lauderdale, Florida	10 Days	Fort Lauderdale, FL, Philipsburg, Castries, Soufriere, Bridgetown, Roseau, Cabrits, St Thomas, Nassau, Fort Lauderdale, FL	$2380–7240
April 23, 1995	Ft Lauderdale, Florida	15 Days	Fort Lauderdale, FL, Oranjestad, Cartagena, San Blas Island, transit Panama Canal, Puerto Quetzal, Acapulco, Cabo San Lucas, Los Angeles, CA	$3575–13450
May 14, 28, **June** 11, 25, **July** 9, 23, **August** 6, 20, **September** 3, 1995	Vancouver, British Columbia	7 Days	Vancouver, BC, Inside Passage, AK, Ketchikan, AK, Juneau, AK, Sitka, AK, Hubbard Glacier, AK, Valdez, AK, Seward, AK	$1530
May 21, **June** 4, 18, **July** 2, 16, 30, **August** 13, 27, **September** 10, 1995	Seward, Alaska	7 Days	Seward, AK, Valdez, AK, Hubbard Glacier, AK, Sitka, AK, Juneau, AK, Ketchikan, AK, Inside Passage, AK, Vancouver, BC	$920
September 17, 1995	Vancouver, British Columbia	7 Days	Vancouver, BC, Inside Passage, AK, Ketchikan, AK, Juneau, AK, cruise Glacier Bay, Sitka, AK, Inside Passage, AK, Vancouver, BC	$1530
October 3, 1995	Vancouver, British Columbia	18 Days	Vancouver, BC, San Francisco, CA, Cabo San Lucas, Acapulco, Puerto Caldera, transit Panama Canal, Willemstad, Ocho Rios, Fort Lauderdale, FL	$4085–14145
October 5, 1995	San Francisco, California	16 Days	San Francisco, CA, Cabo San Lucas, Acapulco, Puerto Caldera, transit Panama Canal, Willemstad, Ocho Rios, Fort Lauderdale, FL	$3785–13845
October 10, 1995	Acapulco, Mexico	11 Days	Acapulco, Puerto Caldera, transit Panama Canal, Willemstad, Ocho Rios, Fort Lauderdale, FL	$3245–11870

Figure 5.24 Sailing schedules.

QUICK CHECK!

1. Your clients want to sail on one of Holland America Line's newer ships, the *Ryndam.* Their vacation is for two weeks at the beginning of March.

   Where is this ship departing from at that time of year? _____.

   How long is the cruise?_____.

2. What are the ports of call? _____

3. What is the price range for a cabin per person, based on double occupancy? $_____

4. In which cruise area does the *Ryndam* operate seven-day cruises during the summer months? _____

Port-to-Port Ferry Schedules A port-to-port index of the sailing schedules of several ferry operators, arranged by port of departure with days and times of each crossing (Figure 5.25).

QUICK CHECK!

1. Your client plans to take a cross-channel ferry between Dover, England, and France.

   a. What is the name of the port in France? _____

   b. What is the name of the ferry/cruise company that operates cross-channel crossings? _____

   c. How long does it take to cross? _____

   d. What is the fare (in pounds)? £ _____

   e. Your client plans to travel in the summer. What can you say about the frequency of trips during the early to mid-afternoon? _____

2. How long is the ferry ride between Copenhagen, Denmark, and Oslo, Norway? _____

3. Scandinavian Seaways offers daily departures between Copenhagen and Oslo.

   What is the departure time during the summer? _____

   How much does it cost? $_____

COPENHAGEN, DENMARK

To: Oslo, Norway   *Cruise Company: Scandinavian Seaways*

Days of Departure	Departure Time	Length of Crossing	Fare
Daily	17:00*	16 hours	$79.00

*No sailings Apr 18, 20, 22; Jan 1 transit time 17 hr

To: Swinoujscie, Poland   *Cruise Company: Polish Baltic Shipping Co*

Days of Departure	Departure Time	Length of Crossing	Fare
MTThFSu	11:00 (Su); 21:30 (xSu)*	10 hours, 15 minutes	$80.00

*No sailings Jan 2, Apr 3, Dec 25, 26

DOVER, ENGLAND

To: Calais, France   *Cruise Company: P & O European Ferries*

Days of Departure	Departure Time	Length of Crossing	Fare
Daily (Jan 1–Dec 24, Dec 27–31)	01:00; 03:00; 04:00; 05:00; 05:45*; 06:30; 08:00; 08:45; 11:00; 12:30; 13:15; 14:00; 14:45*; 15:30; 17:00; 17:45; 18:30†; 19:15*; 20:00†; 21:30†; 22:15†; 23:00†; 23:59	75 minutes	£25.00

*Only Feb 17–27, Apr 11–Sep 24
†No sailing Dec 24

Dec 26, 1995	08:00; 09:30; 12:30; 14:00; 17:00; 18:30; 21:30; 23:00	75 minutes	£25.00

Figure 5.25 **Port-to-port ferry schedules.**

Ship Profiles   This is the most extensive section of this resource, listing over 350 vessels by type—Cruise Ships, Destination/Expedition Cruises, Masted Sailing Ships, River Cruises, and Ferries/Freighters/Day Cruises. There is a lot of information regarding each ship, including the following:

- *The basics*—Ship name, dates built and refurbished, former name, and country of registry.
- *Ship particulars*—Technical and otherwise: length, beam, speed, GRT, nationality of officers and crew, size of crew, language(s) spoken by crew, number of cabins, space ratio per passenger, passenger capacity, and whether the ship is stabilized.

- *Client profile*—A general idea of who's on board in terms of singles, couples up to age 35, couples ages 35–55, couples over 55, and families.
- *Tipping and payment policies*—Guide to tipping on board and type of payment accepted on board ship (cash, personal check, credit cards).
- *Description*—Describes accommodations, dining/entertainment, facilities, and services.
- *Sailing schedule/itineraries*—General cruising areas, types of cruises. Will reference other pages in the resource for additional information.

Checkpoint 5.7 _____

Refer to Figure 5.26, a sample page from the "Ship Profiles" section, and answer the following questions.

1. When was the *Majesty of the Seas* built?_____

2. What is the name of the cruise line that operates this ship?

   _____

3. You want to make reservations for your clients on the *Majesty of the Seas*. What number would you call if your office is in Boston?

   _____

4. Your clients are asking if this is a spacious ship; they don't want to wait in lines all the time! What is the space ratio on this ship? _____ (*Hint*: This is already calculated for you in this section.) Would you consider it a spacious ship for these passengers? _____

5. How many passenger decks are there?_____

6. How many total cabins are there? _____

7. Does this ship have facilities for the handicapped? _____

8. Which choice most accurately describes the typical passenger?
   a. couples over age 55   c. families
   b. singles   d. couples up to age 35

9. Each ship provides tipping guidelines. Your clients are sailing on the *Majesty of the Seas* on a seven-day cruise. Since this is their first cruise, they want to know how much they should expect to tip at the end of the cruise. Using the *Majesty's* guidelines, what would be the total for two adults to tip the cabin steward, waiter, and busperson?

   $_____

MAJESTY OF THE SEAS

Built: **1992**
Country of Registry: **Norway**

ROYAL CARIBBEAN INTERNATIONAL

1050 Caribbean Way, Miami, FL 33132 Tel: 305-539-6000 Fax: 305-374-7354
Reservations: In USA 800-327-6700; for groups 800-722-5476.

Deck Plans, Pages 210 & 211

SHIP SPECIFICATIONS

LENGTH in ft.	BEAM in ft.	SPEED in knots	STABILIZED
880	106	19	Yes

GRT in cu. ft.	OFFICERS' NATIONALITY		CREW'S NATIONALITY
73,941	International		International

LANGUAGES SPOKEN BY CREW		SIZE OF CREW	ELEVATORS
Multilingual		827	11

PASSENGER DECKS	TOTAL CABINS	SPACE RATIO PER PASS. in cu. ft.	
14	1177	31.4	

REGULAR PASSENGER CAPACITY		TOTAL PASSENGER CAPACITY	
2354		2744	

FACILITIES FOR THE HANDICAPPED

2 outside and 2 inside cabins with ramp access and 5-foot turning radius in bathroom and bedroom, flat floors and folding seat in showers.

CLIENTELE PROFILE

TYPE	%0	10	20	30	40	50	60	70	80	90	100
Singles											
Couples to 35											
Couples 35-55											
Couples over 55											
Families											

TIPPING GUIDELINES

(PER PERSON PER DAY UNLESS OTHERWISE NOTED)

Cabin Steward		$3	Deck Steward	— — —
Maitre d'	Discretionary		Waiter	$3
Wine Steward	Discretionary		Bus Boy	$1.50

TYPE OF PAYMENT ACCEPTED ON BOARD

Cash	No	Checks	No	On-Board Charge System	Yes
Credit Cards	American Express, Diner's Club, Discover, MasterCard, Visa				

DESCRIPTION

This sister ship to Monarch of the Seas and Sovereign of the Seas entered service in 1992 as one of the grandest ships afloat, maintaining the fine tradition of her fleet.

Accommodations

Spacious staterooms equipped with private shower, air conditioning, closed-circuit TV, radio, phone and closet; some with tub and VCR — 12 Suites with marble bath, terry robes, sitting area, bar and private balcony — Family

Suites — 110AC/60DC Power — 24-hour Room Service.

CABIN TYPE	No. INSIDE	No. OUTSIDE	SIZE in sq. ft.
Suites	0	12	264-670
Double/Queen Bed	0	0	—
With 2 Lowers	301	630	119-122
Convert to Doubles	0	630	119-122
Upper & Lower	0	90	—
Single Lower Only	0	0	—
TOTALS	445	732	

Dining/Entertainment

DINING ROOMS	SEATING
Mikado Dining Room (Theme meals)	706
Maytime Dining Room (Theme meals)	666
Windjammer (Buffets, Continental cuisine)	900

Number of seatings for dinner: 2 — Hours: 6:15 & 8:30 pm

Fine French, Italian, Caribbean and Continental cuisine served in the Mikado and Maytime Dining Rooms — Breakfast and lunch buffets in the Windjammer Cafe — A Chorus Line Lounge presents the ship's main shows — Live music in the Paint Your Wagon Lounge and the Blue Skies Lounge — The On Your Toes Nightclub features dance music — Schooner Bar with piano entertainment — Viking Crown Lounge — Intimate 55-seat Touch of Class Champagne Bar — Casino Royale.

Facilities/Services

Aerobics and Exercise Classes — Gym and Jogging Track — 2 Outdoor Pools, 2 Whirlpools, 2 Saunas and Massage — Shuffleboard, Ping-pong, Horseracing and Basketball — Backgammon, Bridge and Bingo — Snorkeling Instruction — Babysitting, Counselors, Game Room, Playroom and Teen Activities — Hairdresser — Duty-free Shops, Boutique, Liquor Store and Photo Shop — Library — Writing Room — Meeting Room to 100 — Tour Office — Laundry — Dry Cleaning — Currency Exchange — Medical Facilities.

SAILING SCHEDULE

7-night cruises of western Caribbean (including Mexican ports), leaving on Sundays. **Double occupancy rates per person range from $1329 to 3999. For detailed itinerary, see page 685. For booking information, see page 39.**

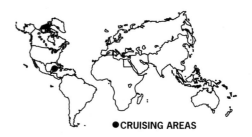

●**CRUISING AREAS**

Figure 5.26 Ship profiles.

10. When the passenger purchases items in the shops on board, will the shops accept personal checks? _____

11. This ship has an onboard charge system. During the first day or two of the cruise, each passenger gets an onboard "charge card" that is used to make all onboard purchases. This includes drinks in the bars and purchases in the ship's shops. At the end of the cruise, the passenger gets a total bill. The ship accepts five types of credit cards for payment of the total bill at the end of the cruise. Which cards are accepted?

_____ _____ _____

_____ _____

12. How many suites with private balconies does this ship have? _____

13. Are there TVs in each cabin? _____

14. What are the names of the two main dining rooms?

_____ _____

15. Which is the larger dining room in terms of seating? _____

16. What time is the early seating for dinner? _____ the late seating? _____

17. In which area are breakfast and lunch buffets served? _____

18. How many outdoor pools does this ship offer? _____

19. Your clients will be bringing their young children on board. Are there activities and/or counselors for them? _____

20. This ship offers seven-day cruises to the _____ Caribbean. Rates based on double occupancy range from $_____ to $_____ per adult.

THE CLIA MANUAL

The Cruise Lines International Association (CLIA) consists of 33 member cruise lines and more than 20,000 travel agency affiliates. CLIA's main objective is to market and promote cruise vacations to the traveling public in addition to offering educational and training support to its member travel agencies to assist them in selling cruise travel.

One of the association's major publications is the CLIA *Manual*, published on an annual basis and sold to travel agencies as a resource. It is similar to the *Official Cruise Guide* because it contains detailed descriptions of cruise ships. The main difference, however, is that the CLIA *Manual* is a lot

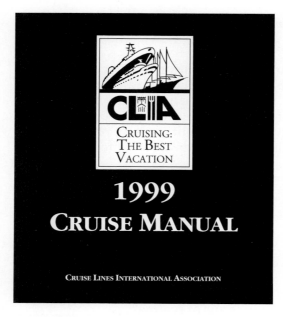

Figure 5.27 The CLIA *Manual*.

more visual in nature: it contains deck plans, sample menus and wine lists, examples of daily activity sheets for passengers, and much more.

When you read this manual for the first time, you will notice that everything is printed in black and white. How does this help you? Deck plans and other graphics in this manual can easily be photocopied for your clients before their trip. It's a nice touch to send your clients a deck plan of the ship with their cabin circled, sample menus, and whatever else you can find for them to help them prepare for their cruise vacation.

To show you the versatility of this particular resource, we have included several sample pages from this manual.

The CLIA *Manual* is divided into three major sections: CLIA cruise company data, ship profiles, and general information.

CLIA Cruise Company Data

For each CLIA company represented, the following information is provided:

- Sales policies (Figure 5.28)
- Sales personnel
- List of ships

Figure 5.28 shows a sample page from the "Sales Policies" section.

Ship Profiles

Specific information regarding each ship is provided, including:

- Size and capacity
- Accommodations (number of outside/inside cabins, number of suites)
- Public rooms and capacity
- Facilities and services

Figure 5.29 shows a sample page from this section for Carnival Cruise Lines' *Holiday*.

General Information

This section contains a compendium of useful information for the sales agent, including:

- Embarkation port maps (Figure 5.30)
- Destination details
- Cruise guide grids for honeymooners, wheelchair users, children, and active adults. (Figure 5.31)
- CLIA promotional materials (for sales agents)

Checkpoint 5.8 _____

Answer the following questions by referring to the sample pages from the CLIA *Manual* (Figures 5.28, 5.29, 5.30, and 5.31).

1. Your clients, a party of two, are sailing on a Carnival Cruise Lines seven-day vacation.
   a. What is the total amount of deposit that is required? _____
   b. How many days before departure is final payment due? _____
2. What is the standard percentage of commission a travel agency earns when booking a Carnival cruise?_____
3. Your clients are sailing on Carnival Cruise Lines' *Holiday*.
   a. What is the total passenger capacity if all accommodations plus upper berths are occupied? _____

SALES POLICIES

- **Deposits —**

  $200 per person, 7 day cruises;
  $100 per person, 34 day cruises.

- **Final Payment —**

  Due 45 days prior to sailing.

- **Level(s) of Commission —**

  10% normal commission/15% to Florida Agents on cruise only business.

- **Agent's reduced fares —**

  Space Available Agent's Rate: CLIA, $25.00 per person per day plus port charges. Non-CLIA, $35.00 per person per day plus port charges. *Positive Space* Agent's Rate: 50% discount off brochure rate plus port charges. *Reduced Rate* fares are available only to agent and family members in cabin.

- **Group concessions —**

  * One free tour conductor pass for every 15 full-paying adult passengers. (No limit.) Fly Aweigh package includes air tick et for tour conductor(s).
  * 10% group discount year round except holiday sailings on cruise only groups. (Cat. 4-12 only.)
  * 5% group discount on Fly Aweigh groups year round. (Cat. 4-12 only.) Additional 5% to 15% discount available on selected sailings.

- **Air/Sea Arrangements —**

  Fly Aweigh: All inclusive air/sea program available for all itineraries from over 175 cities, featuring ''Free Air'' from most markets. Optional tour packages available upon request.

- **Cooperative Advertising —**

  Available on a 50/50 basis for *retail* promotions approved in advance.

- **Charters —**

  Rates are available upon request for partial charters and full ship charters.

- **Single Occupancy Rate —**

  150/200% depending on the category selected.

- **Double Occupancy Cabins offered on a share basis —**

  Yes. Guarantee of sailing date given at booking, cabin category to be assigned by Carnival Cruise Line.

- **Credit Cards —**

  Yes, on-board purchases and casino.

Executive Offices:
(800) 327-7373
(305) 599-2600

Cable: Cruiseship
Telex: 519206

Carnival Cruise Lines

5225 N.W. 87th Avenue, Miami, Florida 33166

Figure 5.28 Sample page from the "Sales Policies" section.

NAME: HOLIDAY
COMPANY: CARNIVAL CRUISE LINES
ORIGINALLY BUILT: 1985
COUNTRY OF REGISTRY: PANAMA
SPEED: 21 KNOTS
NORMAL CREW SIZE: 660
NATIONALITY OF CREW
    OFFICERS: ITALIAN
    HOTEL STAFF: INTERNATIONAL
    CRUISE STAFF: INTERNATIONAL

SIZE/CAPACITY

GROSS REGISTERED TONNAGE: 46,052
LENGTH: 728 FEET   **BEAM:** 92 FEET
TOTAL CAPACITY (Incl uppers): 1760
NORMAL CRUISE CAP. (Basis 2): 1452
SPACE RATIO 32

ACCOMMODATIONS

TYPE	No. Outside	No. Inside
SUITES† *	10	
TWINS*	433	250
UPPERS/LOWERS	10	23
TOTAL	453	273
TOTAL CABINS	726	

* All convert to king size beds.
† Include bathtub jacuzzis.

PUBLIC ROOM CAPACITIES

NAME	Capacity
FOUR WINDS DINING ROOM	356
SEVEN SEAS DINING ROOM	482
AMERICANA LOUNGE	700
BLUE LAGOON	492
TAHITI LOUNGE	114
REFLECTIONS DISCOTHEQUE	175
RICK'S CAFE AMERICAN	81
CARNEGIE LIBRARY	40
CAPUCCINO'S BAR	45
THE BUS STOP	
THE BUS STOP BAR	
GAMING BAR	60
GAMING CLUB CASINO (standing room)	200+
ELECTRONIC GAME ROOM	
LIDO (Outdoor) PATIO BAR & POOL	150
LIDO (Indoor) THE WHARF	335
CHILDREN'S PLAYROOM	30
CARD AREA Times Square/Union Square (each)	32
ENCLOSED PROMENADE-BROADWAY	

FACILITIES

AIR COND. FULLY	HAIR DRYERS (Allowed)
BARBER SHOP	HOSPITAL
BEAUTY SALON	MASSAGE ROOM
BOUTIQUE	PASSENGER DECKS (9)
CHILD COUNSELLORS (Seasonally)	PHOTO GALLERY
CHILDREN'S PLAYROOM	SAUNA
CLOSED CIRCUIT TV	SHUFFLEBOARD
DRUG STORE	SKEET SHOOTING
DUTY FREE SHOPS	SPAS (2)
ELECTRIC CURRENT (110 AC)	STABILIZERS
ELEVATORS (8)	STEREO IN CABINS
FULL CASINO	SWIMMING POOLS OUTSIDE (3)
GOLF DRIVING PLAT.	TABLE TENNIS
GYMNASIUM (whirlpool)	TELEPHONES
	TOUR OFFICE

Figure 5.29 **Sample page from the "Ship Profiles" section.**

MIAMI

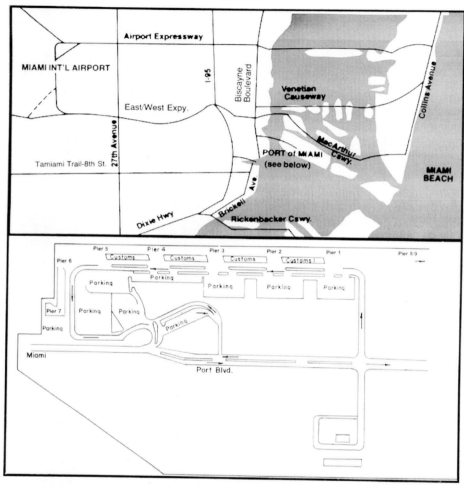

Port of Miami:
Located in Biscayne Bay at the bottom of N.E. 5th St.

Parking Facilities:
Secured parking lots are opposite each pier.

Taxis and Limos:

- To and from Miami International Airport: 20 min. Red Top Limo, $6.00 per person. Phone 305/526-5764

- Taxi rate $12.00-$15.00

- To and from Miami Beach Hotels:
  15-25 min. Red Top Limo, $7.00 per person. Phone: 305/526-5764

- Taxi, So. of 16th St., $ 8.00-$10.00
  So. of 86th St., $ 9.00-$13.00
  No. of 86th St., $13.00-$16.00

- From Downtown Miami hotels, 5-10 min. fare
  $4.00-$5.00
  (All rates approximated)

Berth Assignments:
Each ship sailing out of the port of Miami has a permanent berth assignment. Contact the appropriate cruise line for their assignment(s).

Figure 5.30 Sample embarkation port map.

b. What is the space ratio of this ship? _____

   Is there a lot of elbow room on this ship? _____

c. When was the ship built? _____

d. How many suite accommodations are there?_____

e. How many outside twin-bed cabins are there? _____

f. What type of accommodation includes bathtub Jacuzzis?

   _____

g. There are two dining rooms on board the ship. Which one has the

   larger passenger capacity? _____

h. Name at least four types of passenger recreational or sports facilities
   on board the ship.

   _____   _____

   _____   _____

i. Is there a playroom for children on board? _____

4. Your clients are taking a cruise from the port of Miami. They will be flying to the Miami airport as independent arrivals.

   a. Approximately how much will it cost to take a taxi from the airport

      to the port? $_____

   b. Approximately how long does it take to drive? _____

5. Of the four cruise lines listed, which one offers a children's pool on *all*
   of its ships?
   a. Celebrity Cruises   c. Carnival Cruise Lines
   b. Costa Cruise Lines   d. American Hawaii Cruises

6. Which cruise line offers paddle tennis on only *some* of its ships?
   a. Crystal Cruises   c. American Hawaii Cruises
   b. Costa Cruise Lines   d. Celebrity Cruises

7. Which of the following activities is not offered by Crystal Cruises?
   a. jogging   c. aerobics
   b. masseuse   d. snorkeling lessons

8. Which cruise line offers the least honeymoon features and amenities?
   a. Windstar Cruises   c. Seawind Cruise Line
   b. Silversea Cruises   d. World Explorer Cruises

A: All ships
S: Some ships
H: Only seasonally or whenever children are on board.

	Reduced Cruise Rate (with 1 full time adults) (1)	Air/Sea Rate (same or less as for full fare passengers) (2)	Babysitting Available (2)	Cribs Available (3)	Quad Cabins Available	Arts & Crafts Classes	Basketball	Beach Parties	Bridge Tours	Cartoons	Daily Papers	Dancing Classes	Escorted Shore Tours	Foreign Language Classes	Games & Contests	History & Geo. Classes	Ice Cream Parties	Menus	Movies	Parties	Ping Pong	Pool (Just Kids)	Snorkeling	Teen Center or Disco	Teen Counselors	Video Games	Volleyball	Youth Center/Playroom	Youth Counselors
American Hawaii Cruises	A	A	A	A	A			A		A	A			A	A		H	A	A	A				A	A			A	A
Carnival Cruise Lines	A	A	A	A	A	A		S	A	A	A		A		A	A	A	A	A		S			S	A/H	A	S	S	S/H
Celebrity Cruise Lines	A	A	A	A	A	A	S	S	S/H	A/H	A/H	A		A	S	A/H	A	A	A	A	S		S	A/H	A	S	S	S/H
Commodore Cruise Line	A	A		A	A			A		A			A		A	A	A	A	A			A	A/H	A			A	A/H
Costa Cruise Lines	S	A	A	A	A	A	S	S	A	A	A	S	S	S	S	S	A	S	A	A	A	S	S	S	A	A	A	S	A	A

	Sunday/Monday Departures	Complimentary Champagne/Wine Reception	Complimentary Cake	Flowers	Table for Two	*Double Bed or Equivalent	SPECIAL AMENITIES
Seawind Cruise Line	•	•	•	•	•	•	Certificate, Photo
Seven Seas Cruise Lines	•	•	•	•	•	•	Champagne & Caviar
Silversea Cruises	•	•	•	•	•	•	
Sun Line Cruises	•	•	•		•	•**	
Windstar Cruises	•	•		•	•	•	Certificate can be arranged; Gifts for purchased
World Explorer Cruises	•	•	•	•	•		Card from Captain & Photo

* Available in selected categories/ships **Limited

A: All ships
S: Some ships
I: Information on local facilities provided by ship staff.

	ON-BOARD																				ASHORE*									
	Aerobics	Basketball	Low-Cal Menu Choice	Golf Driving	Gym	Jogging	Masseuse	Paddle Tennis	Sail Boating	Sauna	Scuba Diving	Skeet Trap Shooting	Snorkeling	Snorkeling Lessons	Spa Pool	Swimming	Total Fitness Program	Volleyball	Water Skiing/Jet Skiing	Windsurfing	Bicycling	Charter Fishing	Golf	Hiking	Horseback Riding	Scuba Diving	Snorkeling	Tennis	Water Skiing	Windsurfing
American Hawaii Cruises	A		A		A	A	A		A/I	A	A/I		A/I	A/I		A		A/I	A/I	A/I	A/I	A/I	A/I	A/I	A/I	A/I	A/I	A/I	A/I	A/I
Carnival Cruise Lines	A/I		A	A	A	A		A			A	S	A	S	S				A/I	A/I	A/I	A/I	A/I	A	A/I	A/I	A/I	I		I
Celebrity Cruise Line	A	S	A	S	A	A	A	A	I	A	I	A	I		I	S	A	S	S		I	I	I	I	I	I	I	I	I	I
Commodore Cruise Line	A		A	A	A			A/I	A	A/I		A	A/I	A/I	I	I	I	I	I	I	I	I	I	I	I	I	I	I	I	I
Costa Cruise Lines	A	S	S	S	A	A	A	S		A	S	S	S	S	S	A	A	I	I	I		I	S	S		S	S	S	S	I
Crystal Cruises	A		A	A	A	A	A		A			A	A	A		I		I	I	I	I	I	I	I	I	I	I	I	I	*

Figure 5.31 Sample cruise guide grids.

THE CRUISE BROCHURE

In addition to being an important resource for the sales agent, cruise brochures are also the number one sales tool! The cruise lines realize the importance of the cruise brochure in the selling process. In many cases, the client is sold on a cruise based on the pictures, design, and descriptions contained in a cruise brochure; a poorly designed brochure does little in motivating the client to buy. That is why cruise lines pay a lot of money to produce the most colorful and dazzling marketing pieces printed for the general public.

Most cruise brochures are broken down into the following sections:

- Promotional section
- Itineraries and ports of call
- Cost chart and deck plans
- Booking information and conditions of travel

Promotional Section

Usually, the first few pages of any cruise brochure will contain dazzling pictures and descriptions for promotional purposes only. They are designed to intrigue and motivate the client to buy! These pages usually contain photos of the ship's passengers (many of whom are models) dining, dancing, winning in the ship's casino, or just lounging in deck chairs . . . all with satisfied grins on their faces!

Not only do these photos convey what it is like on board the ship, but they also hint at something very important. Usually you can tell the average age of the ship's passengers by noting who is posing for the brochure's pictures. If the brochure features families with children, the cruise line is sending a signal to the buyer that children are welcome and activities are available for that age group. If the passengers appear somewhat older and more sophisticated, the ship is targeting more mature, upper-income, experienced travelers who are looking for a high level of service and luxury.

Itineraries and Ports of Call

One of the most important factors in choosing a cruise is the ship's itinerary and ports of call. Cruise lines will always feature their itineraries in brochures, along with a description and pictures of the ports visited.

Cost Chart and Deck Plans

Each brochure will contain a cost chart. The cost chart is divided into cabin categories, usually from most to least expensive. Each category is identified by a letter or number. Cabins for each category are also described in terms of deck location and whether they are outside or inside. Each category is also color-coded and cross-referenced with the deck plans for easy identification.

Booking Information and Conditions of Travel

This important section is usually printed on the back pages of the brochure. It contains important information regarding ship procedures, policies, reservation and deposit requirements, cancellation policies, and documentation requirements. Important information for both the travel agent and client is noted here and should be read and understood thoroughly!

Figure 5.32 is a reprint from a cruise brochure for Costa Cruise Lines' *CostaRiviera*.

THE INTERNET MAKES WAVES

The Internet, the world's largest network of computers, is becoming a major force in the travel industry, from the perspective of both users and travel companies. According to a recent U.S. travel agency survey conducted by *Travel Weekly*, approximately 25 percent of travel agencies access the Internet, and the number is growing every day.

How do travel professionals use the Internet? Fewer than you would expect use it to make bookings for clients—only 23 percent use it for that purpose. Instead, a whopping majority—60 percent—use the Internet to gather product and destination information for their clients.

Years ago, finding travel sites on the Internet was a challenge. Today there are hundreds of them—travel agencies, airlines, hotels, tour operators, car rental companies, trade publications—and more are being added each day. Cruise-only agencies as well as the major cruise lines themselves are using the Internet to reach hundreds of thousands of potential clients at a fraction of the cost of traditional promotional materials. With just a point-and-click, users can view deck plans, see what a typical cabin looks like, or read a typical menu on selected ships. They can also find out which ships are family-friendly and which target the upscale adventurer. It's like reading through dozens of printed brochures by just pointing-and-clicking your way through colorful pictures and video presentations of selected cruise vacations right on your home computer screen. There are also Web sites that list cruise discounts and bargains—information difficult to obtain by just reading the cruise brochure and printed resources.

A growing number of travel agencies are adding the Internet to the other resources found in the workplace. After all, as a travel professional, you should have access to the same information about cruise ships and discount programs that your clients now have in their own homes!

Figure 5.32 A sample cruise brochure.

THE SOUTHERN
CARIBBEAN CRUISE
WITH AN ITALIAN
ACCENT.

CostaRiviera's Italian-style service sets the mood for a week of carefree adventure. In no time at all, you'll feel like part of a big, fun-loving family. There's the crew-member who greets you like an old friend and escorts you to your stateroom on boarding day. The cabin steward who seems to know, without being asked, when you'd like coffee or an extra pillow. The irrepressible cruise director who keeps the good times going from morning until long into the night.

And of course, there are Costa's legendary chefs – trained in Europe and members of the prestigious Chaine des Rotisseurs – who make every meal an event worth remembering.

Feast on freshly baked breads and delicate home-made pasta. Tender beef, Caribbean seafood and expertly prepared Italian specialties like Ossobuco alla Milanese.

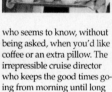

3

Figure 5.32 (*continued*)

**EIGHT DESTINATIONS
IN SEVEN
UNFORGETTABLE DAYS.**

Your Southern Caribbean adventure begins in San Juan, Puerto Rico. The ship departs at midnight on Saturday – leaving plenty of time to enjoy the beautifully preserved Old San Juan historic district, and to get a taste of the city's famous nightlife. Then board the CostaRiviera for a warm Italian welcome, and make yourself at home in a spacious stateroom.

You'll awaken on Sunday morning at St. Thomas, the Caribbean's premier yachting destination. Bargain for duty-free treasures in the lovely town of Charlotte Amalie, or take a ferry excursion to St. John and the Virgin Islands National Park.

Spend Monday on the French island of Martinique, with its towering rain forest, volcanic peaks, chic resorts and colorful creole fishing villages. And return to your ship in time for a grand Italian dinner.

Tuesday is a thoroughly relaxing cruise day. Sleep late, then help yourself to a

bountiful breakfast buffet. Explore the intriguing little shops of the piazzetta. Work out at SpaCosta, unwind in one of three Jacuzzis®, and cool off in the swimming pool. Then settle into a deck chair to await the sunset with an icy tropical cocktail or a glass of good Italian wine.

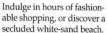

On Wednesday, you'll visit Caracas, the vibrant capital city of Venezuela. Cradled in a valley between mountain ranges, Caracas retains a sense of history as dramatic as its setting. Tour its excellent museums, formal gardens and centuries-old Spanish plazas.

Thursday finds you on sunny Aruba, a sophisticated island of modern resorts contrasted with charming, rainbow-colored Dutch Colonial buildings.

Indulge in hours of fashionable shopping, or discover a secluded white-sand beach.

And on Friday, you are treated to the Caribbean's most unique ports of call, Serena Cay and Casa de Campo. Enjoy either or both for an entire day. A world of privilege, exclusively for guests of the CostaRiviera.

7-DAY SOUTHERN CARIBBEAN ITINERARY
San Juan to San Juan, 10/31/92 - 4/24/93 & 10/30/93 - 12/11/93

DAY	PORT	ARRIVE	DEPART
Saturday	San Juan		Midnight
Sunday	St. Thomas/St. John*	7:00 AM	5:00 PM
Monday	Martinique	11:00 AM	7:00 PM
Tuesday	At Sea	–	–
Wednesday	Caracas	8:00 AM	6:00 PM
Thursday	Aruba	8:00 AM	1:00 PM
Friday	Serena Cay and Casa de Campo	8:00 AM	6:00 PM
Saturday	San Juan	8:00 AM	

*Port of call is St. Thomas with optional excursion to St. John.

6

Figure 5.32 (*continued*)

16-NIGHT CRUISES THROUGH THE PANAMA CANAL.

One exciting week aboard the CostaRiviera is bound to leave you eager for more. Join us again, for Italian-style vacations to some of the world's most intriguing cruise destinations.

Two thrilling 16-night journeys stretch between the Atlantic and the Pacific, encompassing the Caribbean, Central America and Mexico.

Choose a westbound cruise from San Juan to St. Thomas/St. John in the Virgin Islands; Costa's idyllic private island, Serena Cay; Casa de Campo in the Dominican Republic; Aruba, Puerto Caldera, Acapulco, Puerto Vallarta, Mazatlan and Los Angeles. Or cruise eastbound from Los Angeles to Cabo San Lucas, Puerto Vallarta, Acapulco, Puerto Caldera, Aruba, Serena Cay, Casa de Campo, St. Thomas/St. John and San Juan.

Explore Alaska's rugged Inside Passage in Italian-style comfort.

From May 21 to Sept. 17, 1993, CostaRiviera offers 7-day Alaska cruises, sailing roundtrip from Vancouver to rustic Ketchikan, the Endicott Arm, Juneau, Skagway, the Davidson and Rainbow Glaciers, and historic Sitka, once the capital of Russian Alaska. Ask your travel agent for a free brochure.

WESTBOUND ITINERARY: SAN JUAN TO LOS ANGELES
May 1 - May 17, 1993

DAY	DATE	PORT	ARRIVE	DEPART
Saturday	5/1	San Juan		10:00 PM
Sunday	5/2	St. Thomas	8:00 AM	5:00 PM
Monday	5/3	Serena Cay	8:00 AM	5:00 PM
Tuesday	5/4	Aruba	Noon	6:00 PM
Wednesday	5/5	At Sea		
Thursday	5/6	Canal Crossing	7:00 AM	8:00 PM
Friday	5/7	At Sea		
Saturday	5/8	Puerto Caldera	8:00 AM	7:00 PM
Sunday	5/9	At Sea		
Monday	5/10	At Sea		
Tuesday	5/11	Acapulco	9:00 AM	
Wednesday	5/12	Acapulco		2:00AM
Thursday	5/13	Puerto Vallarta	7:00 AM	6:00 PM
Friday	5/14	Mazatlan	8:00 AM	5:00 PM
Saturday	5/15	At Sea		
Sunday	5/16	At Sea		
Monday	5/17	Los Angeles	8:00 AM	

EASTBOUND ITINERARY: LOS ANGELES TO SAN JUAN
September 28 - October 14, 1993

DAY	DATE	PORT	ARRIVE	DEPART
Tuesday	9/28	Los Angeles		4:00 PM
Wednesday	9/29	At Sea		
Thursday	9/30	Cabo San Lucas	Noon	6:00 PM
Friday	10/1	Puerto Vallarta	Noon	6:00 PM
Saturday	10/2	Acapulco	7:00 PM	
Sunday	10/3	Acapulco		6:00 PM
Monday	10/4	At Sea		
Tuesday	10/5	At Sea		
Wednesday	10/6	Puerto Caldera	8:00 AM	7:00 PM
Thursday	10/7	At Sea		
Friday	10/8	Canal Crossing	6:00 AM	5:00 PM
Saturday	10/9	At Sea		
Sunday	10/10	Aruba	9:00 AM	7:00 PM
Monday	10/11	At Sea		
Tuesday	10/12	Serena Cay	8:00 AM	5:00 PM
Wednesday	10/13	St. Thomas	9:00 AM	7:00 PM
Thursday	10/14	San Juan	8:00 AM	

7

Figure 5.32 (continued)

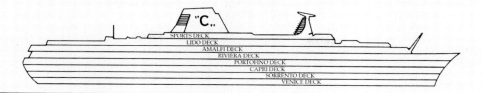

Venice Deck

COSTARIVIERA All rates are per person, double occupancy		INCLUDING AIRFARE		
CATEGORIES & DECKS	**DESCRIPTION OF ACCOMMODATIONS**	**Economy Season** Oct. 31-Dec. 12, 92 Jan. 9, 1993	**Value Season** Jan. 16-Jan. 23, 93 Apr. 3-Apr. 24, 93	**Peak Season** Dec.19-Dec. 26, 92 Jan. 30-Mar. 27, 93
14 Amalfi/Portofino	Deluxe outside, queen bed	$1,895	$1,995	$2,095
13 Amalfi/Portofino	Deluxe outside, 2 lower beds	1,845	1,945	2,045
12 Amalfi/Portofino	Outside, 2 lower beds†	1,795	1,895	1,995
11 Portofino	Outside, 2 lower beds†	1,745	1,845	1,945
10 Capri	Outside, 2 lower beds†	1,695	1,795	1,895
9 Capri/Sorrento	Outside, 2 lower beds†	1,645	1,745	1,845
8 Amalfi/Portofino	Inside, 2 lower beds or queen bed	1,595	1,695	1,795
7 Amalfi/Porto/Capri	Inside, 2 lower beds or queen bed†	1,545	1,645	1,745
6 Capri	Inside, 2 lower beds†	1,495	1,595	1,695
5 Sorrento	Inside, 2 lower beds†	1,445	1,545	1,645
4 Venice	Inside, 2 lower beds†	1,395	1,495	1,595
3 Portofino/Capri	Outside, 1 lower, 1 upper bed	1,195	1,295	1,395
2 Capri/Sorrento	Inside, 1 lower, 1 upper bed	1,095	1,195	1,295
1 Venice	Inside, 1 lower, 1 upper bed	995	1,095	1,195
	Single occupant	150% of applicable rate		
	Third/Fourth Adult	795	795	795
	Third/Fourth Child	695	695	695
	Port tax & service charge	76	76	76
	Internat'l Departure Tax/U.S. Gov't. Federal Excise Tax/Customs & Immigration User's Tax	6/3/10	6/3/10	6/3/10

All rates in U.S. dollars. †Cabins available with one or two additional beds.

Air Travel: Prices above include round-trip airfare to San Juan from selected cities. If you do not require airfare, you may deduct $400 from the cruise price.
Holiday Supplement: $150 per person (Christmas and New Year's).
Pre- and Post-Cruise Tours: For details, see page 11.
Air/Sea Information: For details, see page 10.

BOOK EARLY AND SAVE!
Book any 1992 or 1993 Caribbean cruise aboard the CostaRiviera 60 days in advance and receive a $250 discount
on categories 4-8, and a $350 discount on categories 9-14.

Discounts are per person, based on double occupancy. May not be combined with group or promotional fares or any other discount.

Costa Cruise Lines offers comprehensive travel insurance. See your travel agent for details.

8

Figure 5.32 (*continued*)

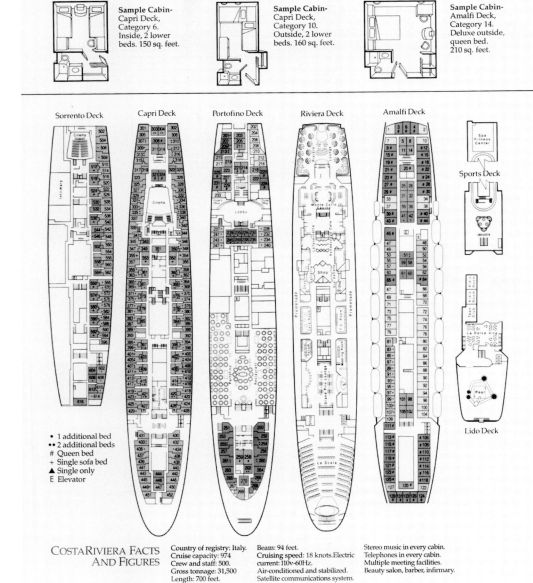

Sample Cabin-
Capri Deck,
Category 6.
Inside, 2 lower
beds. 150 sq. feet.

Sample Cabin-
Capri Deck,
Category 10.
Outside, 2 lower
beds. 160 sq. feet.

Sample Cabin-
Amalfi Deck,
Category 14.
Deluxe outside,
queen bed.
210 sq. feet.

Sorrento Deck

Capri Deck

Portofino Deck

Riviera Deck

Amalfi Deck

Spa
Fitness
Center

Sports Deck

Lido Deck

• 1 additional bed
•• 2 additional beds
Queen bed
+ Single sofa bed
▲ Single only
E Elevator

COSTARIVIERA FACTS
AND FIGURES

Country of registry: Italy.
Cruise capacity: 974
Crew and staff: 500.
Gross tonnage: 31,500
Length: 700 feet.

Beam: 94 feet.
Cruising speed: 18 knots.Electric
current: 110v-60Hz.
Air-conditioned and stabilized.
Satellite communications system.

Stereo music in every cabin.
Telephones in every cabin.
Multiple meeting facilities.
Beauty salon, barber, infirmary.

9

Figure 5.32 (*continued*)

AIR/SEA INFORMATION

COSTARIVIERA'S 1992-93 RATES INCLUDE FREE ROUND-TRIP AIR FROM THESE GATEWAY CITIES:

GATEWAYS

Albany, NY
Allentown/Bethlehem/
    Easton, PA
Amarillo, TX
Asheville, NC   from Char NC/Atl
Atlanta, GA
Augusta, GA
Austin, TX
Baltimore, MD
Baton Rouge, LA
Binghamton, NY
Birmingham, AL
Boise, ID   from Denver
Boston, MA
Buffalo, NY
Cedar Rapids, IA
Charleston, SC
Charlotte, NC
Chicago, IL   O'Hare
Cincinnati, OH
Cleveland, OH
Columbia, SC
Columbus, OH
Corpus Christi, TX   from Dal/Hous
Dallas/Ft. Worth, TX
Dayton, OH
Denver, CO
Des Moines, IA
Detroit, MI
Erie, PA
Fresno, CA   from LAX/SFO
Ft. Lauderdale, FL   from Miami
Ft. Wayne, IN
Greensboro/
    Winston-Salem, NC
Greenville/
    Spartanburg, SC   from Char NC/Atl
Harrisburg, PA   from Philadelphia
Hartford, CT
Houston, TX
Huntsville, AL
Indianapolis, IN
Islip, Long Island, NY from JFK
Jackson, MS
Jacksonville, FL
Kansas City, MO
Knoxville, TN
Las Vegas, NV
Lexington, KY
Lincoln, NE   from St. Louis
Little Rock, AR
Los Angeles, CA
Louisville, KY
Lubbock, TX

GATEWAYS

Madison, WI   from Chicago
Memphis, TN
Miami, FL
Milwaukee, WI
Minneapolis/St. Paul, MN
Mobile, AL
Moline, IL
Montgomery, AL
Nashville, TN
Newark, NJ
New Orleans, LA
New York, NY   from JFK
Norfolk, VA
Oklahoma City, OK
Omaha, NE
Ontario, CA   from LA
Orlando, FL
Pensacola, FL
Peoria, IL
Philadelphia, PA
Phoenix, AZ
Pittsburgh, PA
Portland, ME
Portland, OR
Providence, RI
Raleigh/Durham, NC
Reno, NV
Richmond, VA
Roanoke, VA   from Char NC/Ral
Rochester, NY
Sacramento, CA
Salt Lake City, UT
San Antonio, TX
San Diego, CA
San Francisco, CA
San Jose, CA   from SFO
Savannah, GA
Seattle, WA
Shreveport, LA
South Bend, IN   from Chicago
Springfield, MO
St. Louis, MO
Syracuse, NY
Tallahassee, FL
Tampa, FL
Toledo, OH   from Det/Clev
Tucson, AZ
Tulsa, OK
Washington, DC   from Nat'l or Balt
Wichita, KS
Wilkes-Barre/Scranton, PA

CANADA
Montreal, QUE
Toronto, ONT

The air program is limited from each gateway city and is on request within 35 days of departure and may be unavailable.

Air itineraries are subject to schedules and availability and can be finalized no earlier than 30 days before departure.

Group departures may be subject to restrictions. Air transportation is via scheduled or chartered airlines and Costa will choose the carrier and routing from each gateway city. Flight schedules may require you make connections and/or stop enroute. All travel must remain on the ticketed carrier. Airline tickets issued by Costa Tours are highly restrictive and usually cannot be reissued, revalidated or exchanged for another carrier or routing. Costa Tours does not handle seat assignments, boarding passes or frequent flyer requests. Date deviations handled on request basis only. Deviation requests must be received in writing at least 45 days prior to departure. Administrative fee of $25 per person. Any additional costs for deviations if permitted by the airline are at the passengers' expense.

Costa does not control or supervise any airlines and cannot be responsible for airline delays of whatever nature, including (without limitation) strikes, warlike acts, labor unrest, acts of God or any other act even if the tickets were issued by Costa Tours.

Air travel is round-trip to/from San Juan.

10

Figure 5.32 (continued)

GENERAL INFORMATION AND CONDITIONS.

Please read this general information about your cruise and the related conditions. You need to be aware of them before you book your Costa Cruise Lines Program. Your decision to purchase and payment of the deposit for the tour program you select constitutes your recognition of and consent to all of the terms and conditions of this brochure and your travel ticket and vouchers. Your acceptance and the acceptance of those traveling with you of these tickets and vouchers means that you are bound by these terms and conditions.

Reservations. Deposit required:
7-day cruise – $200 per person.
Final payment: Due no later than six weeks prior to sailing.

Cancellation. Cancellations and requests for refunds must be submitted, in writing, to Costa Cruise Lines N.V. (herein referred to as Costa). All documents (deposit receipt or tickets) issued by Costa must be returned before refund can be processed. Cancellation charges, per person, will be assessed as follows:
45-30 days prior to sailing: $100
29-15 days prior to sailing: $175
14-04 days prior to sailing: Refund subject to prior resale of accommodation. If accommodations are resold, or passengers reschedule their cruise to another sailing date (no protection of rates), a cancellation charge of $200 per person will apply. If the passengers cancel the rescheduled sailing, the penalty of the original booking will apply.
Less than 4 days prior to sailing: No refund, 100% penalty.

A $50 additional penalty will be assessed for each airline ticket that has been issued. A $50 administrative fee will be charged for changes to booking after cruise documents have been issued. Cancellation and administrative charges apply to both individual and group passengers.
See page 11 for deposit/cancellation policies for Cruise Tours.

As no exceptions will be made on cancellation charges, it is recommended that passengers secure appropriate cancellation insurance through your travel agent or through Costa.

Above charges do not include cancellation fees which may be applied by air carriers and/or other land service suppliers, which will be assessed in accordance with such suppliers' policies.

Rates include ocean transportation, accommodations and all meals aboard ship.

Rates do not include shore excursions, port taxes, laundry or valet service, or any other items aboard ship of a personal nature such as wines, liquor, beverages and gratuities.

Rates in U.S. dollars, per person, based on double occupancy of accommodations selected, unless otherwise noted.

Travel Documents. All travel documents as well as compliance with Customs requirements are your responsibility. United States and Canadian citizens need proof of citizenship, such as a birth certificate. Naturalized U.S. citizens are advised to carry their naturalization papers. Aliens who are permanent residents of the U.S. must carry their Alien Registration Card and passport. All others must have valid passports and necessary visas. Please check current requirements with your travel agent.

Shore to Ship Calling. The CostaRiviera can be reached by phone while at sea by dialing 1-800-732-2255 (1-800-SEA-CALL) and asking the High Seas Operator for the desired ship. You will only be charged for the actual conversation time after the ship responds.

Baggage. Baggage Handling: There are porters at the airport and the pier, but hand luggage, valuables and breakable items must be handcarried by the passenger. Costa cannot accept responsibility for any personal items nor for any luggage not under Costa's direct care on-board.
Baggage Responsibility: Costa is not responsible for or liable for damage, loss or theft of baggage or personal effects. Claims for baggage loss or damage must be made in writing to the Chief Purser or Pier Manager prior to leaving the disembarkation pier. Costa's liability for such claims is limited as to passage contract.

Travel Insurance. Costa recommends that you purchase travel insurance. A policy has been designed at a low cost especially for Costa and is made available through your travel agent.
This policy covers Trip Cancellation/Interruption, Travel Delay, Medical Assistance and Emergency Transportation, On-site Hospital Payments, Supplemental Health, Baggage Comprehensive, Legal Assistance, Lost Document and Ticket Replacement, Emergency Cash Transfer, and a 24-hour Emergency Message Center.
Detailed information about this policy will be sent to you with both your booking confirmation and invoice. The information explaining this insurance premium will include a statement of benefits, limitations, restrictions and exclusions. The premium, which is non-refundable, will be included on your invoice. If you choose to not take this comprehensive insurance package, you may exclude the amount of the premium from your payment by completing and returning an enclosed form declining this insurance coverage. You must sign and return the waiver form if you do not wish to purchase insurance, with your initial cruise payment. The insurance is not in effect until Costa has received your premium with your initial cruise payment. Premiums are based on the length of your cruise and are not transferable or refundable. When Costa sends you your travel documents you will be sent a customized insurance brochure which will include an identification card for this policy.

NOTE: THE INSURANCE HAS EXCLUSIONS FOR CERTAIN PRE-EXISTING CONDITIONS. MORE INFORMATION IS AVAILABLE BY CALLING COSTA OR OUR INSURANCE CARRIER.

Departure. Boarding begins at 1 PM in San Juan. All passengers must be aboard no later than one hour before scheduled sailing time.

Services Aboard Ship. Valuables and personal funds should be placed in the safe in the Purser's Office immediately upon embarking. It is recommended that passengers carry traveler's checks and U.S. currency in small denominations No personal checks are cashed aboard ship. Most major credit cards are accepted.
Dining Room table reservations may be assigned by the maitre d' after embarkation.
Deck chairs and cushions are available to all passengers.

Physical/Mental/Medical Disability. Those passengers sailing who have a physical or mental disability, or a medical condition must report same to Costa IN WRITING AT THE TIME THE RESERVATION IS MADE. This information may be forwarded by Costa to the ship's doctor for review.
Failure to provide such information may require Costa to cancel your reservation, prior to the sailing, if sufficient time is NOT provided to make adequate determination of medical condition or requirements.
Costa reserves the right to revoke or refuse passage to anyone who may, in the sole judgment of Costa, require treatment, care or attention beyond that which the ship's facilities can provide or whose medical or physical condition may make them incapable of a cruise voyage. An infirmary, staffed by physician and nurse is available. The doctor is authorized to make customary charges, subject to approval of the ship's Captain, when treating passengers at their request.
Please understand that Costa and its authorized representatives are not liable for any consequence arising from the failure of the travel agent and/or passenger to provide such information. Costa, in accepting a passenger with a physical or mental disability or medical condition, assumes no liability for such passenger beyond that assumed for any other passenger as provided in this brochure. Such passenger is subject to all the limitations and terms and conditions set forth.

Land Packages/Shore Excursions. Shore excursions at moderate extra cost announced in advance on-board will be operated in the various ports of call by local tourist service companies. The tours, hotels, rental cars, sightseeing, shore excursions purchased on board, restaurants and other transportation, whether by air, rail, bus or other means provided by and arranged through Costa, in conjunction with these programs, are not under the control of Costa. The arrangements are made only as a convenience to the passenger. Costa shall not be liable for services and facilities provided by independent contractors resulting in any loss, damage, injury, death or illness nor cost of any delay.

Air/Sea Restrictions. The services of any approved carrier may be used in connection with any of the scheduled or charter tours described herein. Costa reserves the right to utilize such flights and air routings as it, at its sole discretion, may select. Should air/sea passengers choose to change air arrangements, any costs will be at the passengers' expense.

Responsibility and Limitation of Liability. Note once more that your decision to purchase and payment of a deposit for this tour program constitutes your acknowledgement of and consent to all of the terms and conditions of this brochure including the limitations of liability described in it.
In all provision of services other than those on the cruise vessel on which you are traveling, and in accepting arrangements with respect to this tour program, Costa acts ONLY as agent for you or your travel agent in making arrangements for hotels, transportation, shore excursions and all other services rendered with respect to them. Costa expressly disclaims any responsibility for personal injury, property damage, loss, delay inconvenience or other matters due to negligence, wrongful acts, errors or omissions on the part of any supplier of services or goods or of agents selected by you or your travel agent.
The tickets and vouchers issued for this tour program contain further limitations of liability. A statement of these limitations is available to you in advance upon written request. Your acceptance of them constitutes an agreement to all of the terms and conditions stated in the tickets and vouchers. Under these terms and conditions, liability to passengers for damage to or theft of baggage and personal property, delay, personal injury and death as well as other circumstances on board your cruise ship or elsewhere is limited. In addition, your right to recover on a legal proceeding will be based upon the applicable law and forum stated in the ticket voucher. You will find on board your cruise ship, concessions such as shops, photographers, gaming and others. While we may assist you in handling complaints, Costa accepts no responsibility for the actions of these concessions arising from your dealing with them. You must contact and act with them directly.
Costa reserves the right to change or abandon all or any part of the tour program and to change the itinerary whenever advisable or necessary. In this case Costa will NOT be responsible for any loss or expenses caused by reason of such changes or abandonment. If the cruise is withdrawn before sailing date, you shall only be entitled to a refund of the amount received by Costa from you and nothing more. Refunds are not made to passengers who elect not to complete the cruise for any reason or cause whatsoever.

NOTE: Schedules, fares and rates, ports of call, land and flight arrangements and rates are those in effect at time of printing of this brochure. They are all subject to change without notice. You may be required to pay any changes in cost resulting from these items before embarking on the vessel or be denied passage. Once again, we call your attention to the fact that the tickets and vouchers issued for this tour program will contain further limitations of liability. *Read them in advance. If you have any questions about this, call your travel agent or Costa.*

COSTARIVIERA

Italian-style cruising from Europe's leading cruise line. Costa.
Costa Cruise Lines N.V., World Trade Center, 80 S.W. 8th St., Miami, FL 33130-3097

250M 4/92 Inventory #1104 Ship's registry: Italy.

CLIA

Figure 5.32 (continued)

Checkpoint 5.9 _____

Refer to Figure 5.32 and answer the following questions.

1. Your clients are interested in the seven-day Caribbean itinerary during the winter months.

   a. From what port does this ship depart? _____

   b. How many days at sea are there? _____

   c. How long will the ship stay in Caracas? _____

   d. What time does the ship arrive back at the end of the cruise? _____

2. Your clients are confirmed in category 10.

   a. On which deck are these cabins located? _____

   b. Are these cabins inside or outside? _____

   c. Are these cabins available with one additional bed? _____

   d. Your clients want to travel in early February. Is this time considered least expensive (Economy), mid-expensive (Value), or expensive (Peak)? _____

   e. All cruise costs are per person based on double occupancy. What is the cruise cost for a party of two, departing in early February, category 10 (not including airfare or other taxes and fees)? $_____

3. When a passenger is occupying a single cabin, he or she pays a higher rate as compared to a double-occupancy rate. It is normally a certain percentage of the standard rate.

   On the cost chart, find "single occupant." A single passenger must pay 150 percent of the applicable rate. What is the cruise cost for a single passenger occupying a cabin in category 5, departing in November?

   $_____

4. A third or fourth adult occupying a cabin with two other adults will pay a lower cruise cost. It is usually a set cost regardless of the cabin category.

   You have a party of three adults sharing a cabin in category 12, departing December 19 (peak season). What is the cost for:

   a. Each of the first two adults? $_____

   b. The third adult? $_____

   c. All three adults? $_____

5. A family of four (two adults and two children) are occupying the same cabin in category 13, departing October 31 (economy season). What is the cost for:

   a. Each adult? $_____

   b. Each child? $_____

   c. All four passengers? $_____

6. Most cruise lines offer air/sea cruises in which the cost includes both the cruise and airfare from the passenger's home city. Usually all major cities are included. Passengers who purchase the air/sea package must use transportation schedules as provided by the cruise line. Transportation from the airport to the ship is also included.

   Your clients are departing from Boston. Is there free airfare from that city?_____

7. You have booked a seven-day cruise on the *CostaRiviera* for your clients. The cruise line is requiring a deposit within seven days. What is the total amount of deposit for two adults? $_____

8. When is final payment due (how many days or weeks prior to sailing)?

   _____

9. Your clients are booked on a cruise departing April 30. They cancel on April 7 (23 days before departure). What is the cancellation penalty amount for a party of two (no airline tickets or cruise documentation have been issued)? $_____

10. When does boarding begin on the day of embarkation in San Juan?

   _____

CHAPTER REVIEW

1. What does CLIA stand for? _____

2. Who belongs to CLIA and what is its main function?

   _____

   _____

3. What serves as both a cruise resource and an important sales tool?

   _____

4. The different cruise resources share a lot of the same information. However, each one has some unique or special aspects. Next to each type of information or search criterion listed, check the resource that would

best help you in finding the answer (in some case, there may be more than one answer).

Search Criteria	Official Steamship Guide Int'l	Official Cruise Guide	CLIA Manual	Cruise Brochure
1. List of Caribbean cruises embarking from San Juan during the month of April.				
2. Former names of cruise ships.				
3. Color photos and descriptions of ports of call.				
4. List of cruise ships tween 60,000 and 70,000 GRT.				
5. Sample dinner menus.				
6. Ferry schedules between ports all over the world.				
7. Ships that offer special programs such as honeymoon, spa, children, and male hosts.				
8. Terms and conditions, including deposit, final payment, and cancellation policies.				
9. Special theme cruises listed by cruise line.				
10. Typical passenger profile found on a particular cruise ship (age group, single, family, and so on)				
11. Number of outside and inside cabins on a particular ships (quick, at-a-glance).				
12. Deck plan with corresponding cabin categories and prices.				

Sales Techniques 6

After completing Chapter 6, students will be able to:

- Describe two reasons why selling cruises is profitable for travel agencies.

- List five reasons why cruises have one of the highest rates of passenger satisfaction.

- Compare the features and benefits of a land-based vacation in order to validate the value of a cruise vacation to a client.

- Identify and describe the four stages in the cruise sales cycle.

- Define three types of questioning techniques—open, directive, and reflective—and describe how to use them effectively when selling cruise travel.

- Define *feature* and *benefit* and provide examples of each when selling cruise travel.

- Demonstrate the effective use of the cruise brochure during the sales presentation.

KEY TERMS

assumptive close
benefit
choice close
direct close
directive question
feature
open question
reflective question
summary close
valid concern
void concern

- Demonstrate the ability to overcome typical concerns or objections when selling a cruise.

- List and describe the four general steps when dealing with client concerns.

- Describe the four types of closes—assumptive, direct, summary, and choice—by demonstrating a successful closing during a sales situation.

157

*W*HY SELL CRUISES?

There are four major reasons why cruise travel is an important product to sell: profit, passenger satisfaction, potential market, and travel agent services.

It's Very Profitable

A cruise vacation is rewarding to the travel agency. Standard agency commission when booking a cruise is 10 percent. In some cases, travel agencies can earn incentive commissions as high as 18 to 20 percent. Incentive commissions are sales programs offered by cruise companies. Some cruise companies offer incentives based on sales goals; the travel agency must make a minimum number of bookings within a certain time period. Other incentive programs are based on the agency booking specific ships or departure dates. This is an effective way for cruise companies to boost sales during slow or off-peak travel periods.

Selling cruises is also cost effective. It takes one booking to confirm all of the elements of a cruise—airfare, accommodations, meals, entertainment, and transfers. If the agent sells a land-based vacation or puts together an independent tour, many of the elements are booked separately. Also, cruise documentation is prepared by the cruise line and mailed to the travel agency; less time is spent on document preparation. Selling cruises is cost-effective because the travel agency can earn high commissions while spending less time on booking and paperwork.

Passenger Satisfaction

Cruises have one of the highest rates of customer satisfaction compared to other products and services. According to a recent travel industry survey, 85 percent of first-time cruise clients are satisfied and return to book another cruise.

One reason for such a high rate of passenger satisfaction is that cruises are almost totally inclusive; the ship serves as the traveler's accommodations, transportation, restaurant, and entertainment center, all in one package. There is no need for unpacking and repacking at each stop, and no timetables to meet. Since practically everything is taken care of on board the ship, there is less chance of things going wrong such as lost hotel reservations or missing baggage.

Another reason is that clients know the cost of their cruise vacation from the moment they book. Since practically the entire vacation is prepaid, there are few "hidden" or unexpected costs; budgeting the trip is made easier. Also, there is no concern about currency exchange fluctuations that can increase the price of a trip.

Freedom of choice also results in satisfied customers. Cruise passengers have the freedom to do what they want, when they want. When the ship pulls into port, passengers can either chose to go on a variety of shore excursions or just stay on board and relax. Also, there are choices of shipboard entertainment, movies, stage productions, and food to suit practically any taste and style.

Finally, cruise passengers often have special privileges that are not experienced by other travelers. Most cruise ships operate the same itinerary week after week, delivering thousands of potential customers to local shops and attractions at each port of call. Because of the promise of a steady flow of customers, cruise lines have clout when booking shore excursions and visits to local attractions. For example, a shore excursion group may be able to visit an art gallery after hours, or jump to the front of a very long line to get into a world-famous museum.

Potential Market

The potential market for first-time cruisers is huge. Approximately 90 percent of the traveling public has never taken a cruise. An increasing number of people today have the time and money to spend on leisure trips. This is also the time when the "baby-boomers" (roughly between 35 and 60 years of age) have the income and leisure time to travel. Also, there are cruises to fit every budget and vacation period.

Travel Agent Services

Approximately 95 percent of all cruise bookings are made by travel agencies; only 5 percent are made directly by the passenger through the cruise line. This is a much higher percentage than for other types of travel arrangements. For example, approximately 55 and 45 percent of airline and hotel bookings, respectively, are made through travel agencies; the rest are made by the passenger directly with the supplier. The vast majority of travelers seek the assistance of a travel professional when planning and selecting the right cruise vacation for them.

THE SALES CYCLE

There is no script to follow when selling cruises or anything else. Every situation is different; you will never have the same client, being sold the exact same trip, under the same circumstances, more than once! When selling travel, you are dealing with different types of people with a variety of interests, likes and dislikes, expectations, and temperaments. You are dealing with people over the telephone and face-to-face during office visits. You are dealing with serious customers who are ready to make a decision, and with those who are shopping around, looking for the best bargain.

However, there is a sequence of events that should be followed during any sales situation. Successful selling evolves in stages; you can't rush to make a recommendation and ask for a deposit before getting to know who your client is and answering his or her concerns.

The four general steps in a successful sales cycle are:

- *Fact Finding and Qualifying*: Get to know the *who, what, where, when*, and *why*.
- *Presenting and Recommending*: Present selected products that best suit the client.
- *Overcome Objections*: Deal with all client concerns up front.
- *Make the Sale*: Ask for the booking and close the sale.

Step 1: Fact Finding and Qualifying

Who is your client and what are his or her needs? That's the first item on your agenda. You have to understand the needs of the traveler so that you can provide the best product that will meet those needs. You have to go on a fact-finding mission, discover what your clients want, and steer them into making the right decisions.

This first step is also called *qualifying your clients*; you are trying to match them with the best products or service. Qualify is knowing how to ask the right questions and listening effectively to the answers. Asking questions sounds easy, and it is, as long as you follow a few simple guidelines.

Questioning Techniques: The **Hows** *and* **Whos**   Let's first take a look at how to ask questions effectively. Believe it or not, there are many different ways to ask a question. When selling cruises, the three general types of questions are *open, directive*, and *reflective*. The one you use depends on where you are in the sales cycle and what type of response you want.

Open questions do just that: they "open up" your clients so that they will feel at ease and bring out a good deal of information. Open questions do not allow for a simple yes-or-no reply, but will get clients talking about such things as past vacation experiences and their interests and hobbies. Open questions are preferred during fact finding or qualifying because you are trying to gather as much information as possible about your clients at this stage.

Here are some samples of open questions:

"Where did you go on your last vacation? What did you like or dislike about it?"

"What do you like to do during your spare time?"

"Describe your ideal vacation."

Directive questions will require a more focused answer. These questions are used by newspaper reporters when investigating a story; they usually start with words like *who, what, where, when*, and *how*. The client will reply with either a short answer, a choice, or a simple yes or no. These questions should be asked when you have gained a lot of information about your client and now wish to narrow the qualifying process.

Here are some samples of directive questions:

"When do you want to travel?"

"Are you looking for a lot of days at sea, or more ports of call?"

"What ports would you like to visit?"

Reflective questions will provide you with more information based on an answer already provided. These questions are also called *feedback*, because they confirm something that has been said during the conversation. Reflective or feedback probes may ask the client to expand or clarify an answer already provided, or they may "mirror" a response.

Here are some samples of reflective questions:

Client: "We went to Nassau last year on our vacation."

Agent: "Oh, tell me more about it!"

Client: "My wife and I enjoy going to fine restaurants."

Agent: "Good! Tell me which ones."

Listening Techniques: Stop, Look, and Listen   While qualifying clients, not only do you want to ask the right questions, but you have to know how to listen to what your clients are saying! Too often we are concerned with what *we* are saying and how *we* are saying it, and too often we forget to listen.

To employ effective listening techniques, just remember this familiar warning:

STOP—LOOK—LISTEN!

Stop talking and start listening! All too often, we are so concerned with our sales pitch and what we want to say next in the conversation that we tune out what the client is saying. Try not to interrupt at any time. If you have to interrupt in order to keep the conversation on the right track, do it politely by asking another question or repeating what the client has said, to avoid misunderstandings. Remember, the agent should always be in control of the conversation and still remain polite and respectful of the client at all times.

Look to see how your clients are reacting. Don't just listen to what they are saying, but also pay attention to *how* they are saying it and to the nonverbal signals, or *body language*, that they are expressing. According to sales experts, only 7 percent of a person's message is conveyed through words, 38 percent through tone of voice, and 55 percent through body language. This means that 93 percent of what we want to say is not through the words we use but how we say them and how we act.

This means that you have to recognize body language. If you are talking to clients and they lean forward, maintain eye contact with you, and nod and smile at what you are saying, this probably means that they are interested and willing to listen to you. On the other hand, if your clients are leaning back, crossing their arms, not maintaining eye contact, or yawning, this probably means that you have lost their interest or that they feel frustrated or defensive with you.

Listen and tune in to what is being said. The more you listen, the more opportunity you have to discover what your clients want. Tune in to your clients and tune out any distractions that are going on around you. This means tuning out ringing phones, other conversations buzzing around you, and other typical distractions that occur in a busy office. You want to make each client feel that he or she is your most important concern at the moment. Demonstrate that you care by giving your undivided attention and listening closely to your clients.

According to Dean Rusk, best-selling author, "The best way to persuade people is with our ears—by listening to them."

Checkpoint 6.1 _____

Identify each question as open (*O*), directive (*D*), or reflective (*R*) in the space provided.

1. _____ "What are some of the things you like to do on vacation?"

2. _____ "Do you like to play golf?"

3. _____ "What price range do you have in mind?"

4. _____ "You told me that you enjoyed your last cruise to Bermuda. Tell me why."

5. _____ "Have you ever thought of taking a cruise before?"

6. _____ "Are you looking to relax in the sun or to discover new and exciting places?"

7. _____ "Do you want to take a cruise?"

8. _____ "Would you prefer a smaller ship with fewer passengers or a larger ship?"

9. _____ "So you prefer a cruise to Mexico rather than the Caribbean?"

10. _____ "What else would you like to know about this cruise ship?"

The following are directive (yes or no) questions. Many times you will want to ask questions that will provide more information during the qualifying process. Rewrite each question so that the client provides as much information as possible.

11. "Did you like your last cruise on Carnival Cruise Lines?"

_____

12. "Do you enjoy a lot of nightlife?"

_____

13. "Have you thought about where you would like to go on your next cruise?"

_____

14. "Have you ever been to Europe?"

_____

15. "Do you think you would like to try a cruise to a different place, like Antarctica, for example?"

_____

Step 2: Presenting and Recommending

The first step in the sales process is getting to know your client. You have learned that asking the right questions and listening actively to what clients have to say will help you in the initial fact-finding stage. During qualifying, you keep your ideas to yourself! In the next stage, presenting and recommending, you start sharing your ideas with the client.

In the second step, you will present and recommend both the *features* and *benefits* of the cruise product in response to the client's stated needs. In order to make the greatest impact on your clients, focus on what is important to them. This is accomplished by selling cruise *benefits* rather than cruise *features* alone.

Features versus Benefits   Features are tangible—they are the objective and factual aspects of a product. For example, a cruise vacation includes the following features: round-trip transfers, accommodations, entertainment, and meals.

Benefits are intangible—they describe how the client gains or benefits from the product or feature. Benefits are expressed as statements that explain how a product or feature solves a problem, meets a need, or satisfies a desire. The best way to think of a benefit is to put yourself in your client's position and ask yourself, "So what?" or "What's in this for me?" For example, a cruise vacation might include the following benefit statements:

Feature	Benefit
"Round-trip transfers are included."	"This means that you don't have to carry your heavy luggage to the ship; all your baggage is transported directly to your cabin."
"The ship stops in four ports in seven days."	"This gives you a sample of exotic places to explore without the hassle of packing and changing hotels."

If you just use features to sell a cruise, it starts sounding like a laundry list: "This cruise features outside cabins, meals around the clock, entertainment, movies, deck games, gambling . . ." What is important is how each feature will benefit the client. Remember, to turn a feature into a benefit statement, put yourself in the client's place and ask yourself, "So what?" or "What's in it for me?"

Use verbal "bridges" to close the gap between a feature and benefit— first state the feature, use a verbal bridge, then make the benefit statement:

"This cruise line is known for its excellent service." (feature)

"What this means to you is . . ." (verbal bridge)

". . . you never have to cook a meal or make a bed during the entire cruise!" (benefit)

"There is a selection of shore excursions to choose from at each port." (feature)

"This gives you . . ." (verbal bridge)

". . . a lot of choice of what you want to see and do at each destination." (benefit)

Remember, you are selling to client needs. A good way to tell whether you are selling benefits along with features is to apply the "So what?" and "What's in it for me?" test!

Presentation Tips   The following guidelines for effective presentations are suggested by the Cruise Lines International Association (CLIA):

- *Sell to needs.* Stress features and benefits according to the perceived needs of the client.

- *Sell a trip, not a ship.* Establish a cruise experience first, then narrow in on itinerary, cruise line, and ship.

- *Sell by price category.* Start in the middle range (not too high, not too low), if you don't know your client's price range. Work up or down from there.

- *Quote per diem.* To minimize the impact of the total cost of a cruise, quote fares on a per diem basis.

- *Beware the "recommendation."* Be careful with the word *recommendation.* It sounds so final that it may bring a productive dialogue to an end. Make "suggestions" rather than "recommendations" at this point. These allow you to narrow choices and progress toward a final decision. At the same time, they leave you room to maneuver as new needs surface.

- *Be strong and confident!* CLIA market research shows that nearly half of all clients have only a general idea or no idea at all about the vacation they want. They are coming to you—the travel specialist—for advice and suggestions. Don't be reluctant to make some.

The Cruise Brochure: The Sizzle and Steak   The cruise brochure is an important sales tool that travel agents use with clients. The professionally developed cruise brochure has been designed for two major reasons: to excite and to inform. The brochure is a glossy marketing piece; it contains many colorful pictures of the ship with exciting and dramatic descriptions. The brochure is also a guide; it contains booking information such as prices and cabin categories, deposit and final payment terms, and cancellation and refund policies.

Always use the cruise brochure when making a presentation to clients. The following tips will help you use this tool effectively.

For the first-time caller to your office:

- *Don't give away the store!* A common mistake that many travel agents make is to give out too much information at once. Remember, your agency is not an information bureau. If a client calls or comes to your office wanting to take home some brochures, don't give him an armload to sort through! First, qualify the client as much as you can. Based on your perceived needs of the client, select only one or two cruise brochures and explain your choices.

- *Follow it up!* Always get the name, address, and phone number of the person who is inquiring. It doesn't do anyone any good for a potential client to walk out your office door, laden with a bunch of exciting brochures, without any names being exchanged! Always follow up with a phone call and an invitation to come into the office to go over the material.

During the sales presentation in your office:

- *To each his own.* Don't share a brochure with your clients. Each person should have his or her own brochure so that no one has to strain to see.

- *Know when to talk price.* What should you do *first*—turn to the deck plan and prices and talk about cost, or go to the front of the brochure to build excitement about the ship and ports of call? Price should be first. Most people have price on their minds right from the beginning, so deal with it right up front. First turn to the deck plan and price charts at the back of the brochure. Establish price and value. Then use the rest of the brochure and other aids to build interest and enthusiasm about the cruise experience.

Travelers: Why We Picked a Cruise

Factors in Deciding on Cruise Instead of Other Type of Vacation

IMPORTANT FACTORS AND PERCENT OF CRUISERS CITING IT

Destinations/ports of call:	68%
Price/value:	64%
All-inclusive package:	55%
Dining/live entertainment:	46%
Duty-free shopping:	14%
Couples-oriented activities:	14%
Gambling:	12%
Family-oriented activities:	9%
Singles-oriented activities:	8%

Source: New York-based Newspaper Association of America survey of 908 adults who had taken at least one cruise in the last three years. Total exceeds 100% because of multiple responses.

TRAVEL WEEKLY

Figure 6.1 Why travelers choose cruise vacations.

Source: Travel Weekly, reprinted from New York-based Newspaper Association of America survey of 908 adults who had taken at least one cruise in the last three years. Total exceeds 100% because of multiple responses.

- *It's okay to jump around.* Use the brochure to focus on your client's interests, needs, and desires. Don't treat it like a novel, reading it from cover to cover! Skip around and direct attention to those aspects that you know will interest your client. For example, if the client is more interested in the ports of call than in the ship itself, go directly to the itinerary and port descriptions. Skip around the entire brochure like this, touching lightly on sections of lesser interest, and ignoring other sections entirely.

- *Highlight what's important.* While going through the brochure, highlight with a marking pen the important features and benefits in the client's copy. This is helpful to the client when he or she reviews the materials at home. And it serves as a reminder and prompt to contact you with additional questions, or better yet, to make a reservation!

Checkpoint 6.2 _____

For each of the features listed, write a benefit statement you would give to a client in order to focus on his or her needs.

1. Feature: All meals are included.

   Benefit: _____

   _____

2. Feature: An outside cabin is available.

   Benefit: _____

   _____

3. Feature: The ship has both indoor and outdoor pools.

   Benefit: _____

   _____

4. Feature: A post-cruise hotel package is available.

   Benefit: _____

   _____

5. Feature: There are 5 ports of call during your one-week cruise.

   Benefit: _____

   _____

6. Feature: This ship is large and it carries over 1,800 passengers.

   Benefit: _____

   _____

7. Feature: This ship is small, with no more than 600 passengers.

   Benefit: _____

   _____

8. Feature: A variety of different types of travelers and age groups will be on board.

   Benefit: _____

   _____

9. Feature: The total inclusive cost is $1,200.00.

   Benefit: _____

   _____

10. For each client, list the benefits you would use when selling a cruise.

    Susan Brown—a single, young secretary

    _____

    _____

    _____

    Mr. and Mrs. Trulson—a quiet, reserved, middle-aged couple

    _____

    _____

    _____

    Mr. and Mrs. Carleton and their two young children

    _____

    _____

    _____

11. List and briefly describe four useful tips when using a cruise brochure during the sales presentation.

    _____

    _____

    _____

    _____

12. Is it better to mention price or the cruise experience first during the sales presentation? Explain your answer.

    _____

    _____

Step 3: Overcome Objections

No matter how great a salesperson you are, clients will frequently voice concerns or objections about what you are trying to sell them. Concerns are nothing to be afraid of. In fact, you should welcome concerns when you hear them so that you can deal with them at once. The type of objection or concern that you should dread is the one the client hides from you! That's the one that will hurt you the most.

A client can have concerns or objections at any point in the sales process. Don't make a list of them and promise to get back to the client with the answers at a future date. They won't go away. In fact, if you don't deal with concerns on the spot, they will cause a prolonged version or a complete breakdown of the sales cycle.

Void versus Valid Concerns   There are two types of concerns or objections: the void concern and valid concern. The type that is being expressed will determine the best way to handle the situation.

The *void concern* is a misconception that the client has about the product. It is called a void concern because it is not based on anything that is valid or true. Here are some typical void concerns about cruise travel:

"We're in our thirties and too young to go on a cruise!"

"Too much eating all that rich food; I don't want to blow my diet."

"We'll be bored staying on a ship for a week; all day at sea with hardly anything to do."

The best way to deal with a void concern is with correct information. This clears up the client's misconception. For example:

"This ship has people in all age groups. In fact, according to this passenger profile, more than 40 percent of all passengers are under the age of 35!"

"The dining menus on this ship contain 'lean and light' choices; plus they have a great salad bar at lunch on deck! There are aerobics and full-size workout gym facilities available to you."

"This ship has practically everything—from movies and theatrical productions at night to cooking classes, deck and pool games, on-board lecturers, and lots more."

The *valid concern* arises when the cruise does not have a feature that supplies a benefit to the client, or there may be a disadvantage offered by the product or feature. Here are some typical valid concerns about cruise travel:

"Too much sun is not good for you; I shouldn't be out in the sun so much."

"I'm afraid of getting seasick."

"My husband and I are loners and don't like to socialize much while on vacation."

The best way to deal with valid concerns is by stating other benefits. This minimizes and outweighs the disadvantage. For example:

"There are a lot of planned activities and things to do inside the ship during days at sea. Let's take another look at what the ship offers."

"The ship's itinerary is port-intensive; you are at sea for only one day out of a full week. There are many things that can help you with seasickness. Plan a visit to your doctor; I am sure he or she will help you."

"The best feature about this cruise ship is that you have the freedom to participate or not! You can mix with others, but you don't have to. In fact, we can put in a request for a table for two in the dining room."

How to Deal with Concerns A client can express a concern or objection at any time. Deal with it immediately so that you can continue with the sales cycle. Follow these steps when dealing with concerns:

Step 1: Listen actively. As part of the qualifying state, asking questions and listening closely to the client's response is very important. If you hear a concern, establish whether it is void or valid. Also, repeat it back to the client in order to clear up any misunderstanding:

"Are you saying that the price of the cruise is a concern?"

Step 2: Show understanding. Don't become defensive, and certainly don't take a voiced objection personally! Stay in touch with your client's feelings. Show that you have paid attention, and that you certainly understand their concern.

"I understand how you feel."

"I can see why that is important to you."

Step 3: Dispel the concern. Respond to a void concern with education and information; respond to a valid concern with other benefits. Try to back up all that you say with brochures, pictures, or other types of support.

"I can understand your concern about bringing your children on board the ship. This ship has full-time youth counselors that structure activities for children of all ages. Plus, the deck plan shows a separate children's pool and play area, game room, and disco, as some examples."

"I share your concern about eating the right foods. Let me show you some sample dinner menus that will show the 'lean and light' choices available every day."

Step 4: Confirm and move on. Make sure the concern has been cleared up. Look for signs of agreement and acceptance. Always ask to ensure that you have overcome the objection: "Do you feel better knowing that this ship offers a lot to do during the days at sea?"

The Biggest Concern of All: Price The number-one concern of all is probably the total cost of a cruise. The agent should talk not only about how much it is going to cost, but also about what the client is getting for his or her money, or the value of taking a cruise.

Sell value, not price. One of the most effective ways of doing this is to compare a land-based package with a cruise. Land-based vacation packages may appear to be less expensive because they don't have as many inclusive features as cruise vacations have. Make the following comparison for your clients:

CRUISE VACATION VERSUS LAND PACKAGE		
Feature	Typical Cruise	Typical Land Package
Room	Included	Included
Airfare (air/sea)	Included	Included
All meals	Included	Not included
Transporation (*port to port*)	Included	Not included
Sports/recreation	Included	Not included
Entertainment	Included	Not included
Nightclub shows/movies	Included	Not included

Sales Pointer! Be prepared before meeting with your clients. Show a comparison of a seven-day land-based vacation brochure and a seven-day cruise brochure. Compare the inclusive features of both.

Checkpoint 6.3 _____

For each client concern, give the response you would make to handle it.

1. "$1,200 per person is a lot of money for a one-week vacation!"

_____

_____

_____

2. "I don't want to have to eat with the same people, at the same time, at the same table day after day."

_____

_____

_____

3. "What good is it being in an inside cabin without a window during the entire cruise?"

_____

_____

_____

4. "The cabins are too small."

_____

_____

_____

5. "There's too much activity; we just want to relax and not be bothered all the time."

_____

_____

_____

6. "The ship doesn't spend enough time at the ports of call."

_____

_____

_____

Step 4: Make the Sale

All of your qualifying, presenting, and overcoming of concerns are leading to one point—closing the sale. The effective salesperson is also a motivator, gently leading and prodding the client to make a purchase. How do you know when to close the sale? There is no magic signal that will go off like an alarm clock, telling you that your client is ready to make a commitment!

When should you ask for the sale? Feel comfortable in winding up the discussion when any of the following has occurred:

- The client has agreed to a key benefit.
- The client starts asking specific questions regarding a particular item: departure dates, cabin locations, and so on.
- You have answered and resolved all concerns.
- You have justified the cost by demonstrating the *value* of a cruise vacation.
- You recognize strong buying signals from the client.

Buying signals can arise at any time during the sales cycle; you should respond promptly. A typical buying signal is when the client shows signs of approval and agreement with what you are saying: "This cruise sounds great to me!" "Do you think there are any cabins left in our price range?"

Another clear signal is when the client is not asking questions or voicing any concerns. If the client starts making plans by "thinking aloud"—"If we're going to take this cruise to Alaska next month, I'd better see about buying a new camera!"—this may also prompt you to close the sale.

When you know the time is right to close, you may wonder what to say or how to say it. After all, you want to make the client feel comfortable with making a decision, not pressured or bullied into it! There are many different ways of asking for business. Here we will describe four types of closes that work well with cruises: *assumptive*, *direct*, *summary*, and *choice*.

Assumptive Close   Use this type of close when you are sure that your client is ready to buy. This means that you need to read your client's buying signals. If you have done it correctly, you shouldn't receive any resistance.
Here's an example:

Client: "This cruise sounds like a perfect way to relax!"

Agent: "Let's go ahead and check availability for an outside cabin on that departure date."

You have recognized that the client is ready to commit, and assume that a booking is in order. In this case, you are recommending a course of action.

Direct Close   This is similar to an assumptive close. In both cases, the client has displayed a willingness to buy. The difference is that you ask for the booking directly and suggest how to handle some of the details of the booking at the same time.
Here's an example:

Client: "A cruise vacation is looking better and better to me all the time!"

Agent: "I suggest we contact reservations now, set aside the cabin you want, and mail a deposit before the cruise is booked.

The direct close is similar to the assumptive close; however, it is a little more forceful and suggests details of how the booking should be handled.

Summary Close   The summary close is another method to end the sales cycle. Review the features and benefits that were previously discussed, then wrap it up by asking for the sale.

Here's an example:

Client: "This cruise sounds like a good deal."

Agent: "You really get value for your money on this cruise. Remember, everything is included—accommodations, transfers, meals, entertainment, and a wide range of activities. This is a great way for both you and your wife to completely relax and not worry about anything for two full weeks! I am sure the cabin you want is available; all we need to do is to send a deposit to secure it for you."

Choice Close   This is similar to the assumptive close; you offer to book based on the assumption that the client wants to buy. In this case, you give the client a choice, assuming that the client will choose one product or feature over the other.

Here's an example:

Client: "I like the idea of a one-week cruise that includes ports in Mexico."

Agent: "Would you prefer that I book on an outside or inside cabin for you on the cruise to Mexico that departs April 21?"

Checkpoint 6.4 _____

For each client concern, indicate what type of close would be the most appropriate and write what you would say.

1. Your clients, Mr. and Mrs. Amesworth, seem happy about taking a cruise. You have answered all of their questions and concerns.

   What type of close? _____

   What would you say? _____

   _____

2. Your client, Susan Smith, can't make up her mind whether to take a cruise to the Eastern or Western Caribbean.

   What type of close? _____

   What would you say? _____

   _____

3. Your clients, Mr. and Mrs. Plunkett, have never cruised before. You have discussed everything with them, especially their concerns about taking their two young children, the ports of call, and the variety of activities on board the ship. They have no more concerns or questions, but seem to be hesitating.

What type of close? _____

What would you say? _____

_____

CHAPTER REVIEW

1. List four reasons why travel agencies should sell cruises.

_____

_____

_____

_____

2. Name the four steps in the cruise sales cycle:

Step 1: _____

Step 2: _____

Step 3: _____

Step 4: _____

3. Change each yes-or-no question to an open question (which allows the client to provide a lot more information) and a directive question (used to bring out specific information).

Agent: "Did you enjoy your last vacation to Mexico?"

Open: _____

Directive: _____

Agent: "Do you want a seven-day cruise?"

Open: _____

Directive: _____

Agent: "Are just you and your wife traveling?"

Open: _____

Directive: _____

Agent: "Is this cruise within your budget?"

Open: _____

Directive: _____

Agent: "Are you looking for something different on your next cruise?"

Open: _____

Directive: _____

4. What would you say to handle each concern or objection?

Client: "My doctor told me to stay out of the sun."

Response: _____

Client: "My husband and I want to bring the children, but we want some time for ourselves, and we don't think a cruise is the right thing for us."

Response: _____

Client: "I don't want to travel with a lot of old people."

Response: _____

Client: "I don't like the idea of having to eat with the same people day after day."

Response: _____

Client: "I went on a whale-watching cruise for the day and got sick! I don't think a cruise vacation is a good idea!"

Response: _____

Client: "My husband and I want the freedom to do what we want, when we want. A cruise sound too restrictive."

Response: _____

5. For each feature, write a benefit statement.

Feature: All meals are included.

Benefit: _____

Feature: Tips are included in the cost of the cruise on the *Sea Goddess*.

Benefit: _____

Feature: The ship visits six ports on a seven-day cruise.

Benefit: _____

Feature: The ship has several onboard lecturers.

Benefit: _____

6. Why is it sometimes more important to make *suggestions* rather than *recommendations* to a client?

_____

7. List three closing signals that tell you the client is ready to buy.

_____

_____

_____

8. Explain how you would deal with price as a concern when selling cruises. What would you use to support your explanation to the client?

_____

_____

_____

Booking and Documentation 7

PERFORMANCE OBJECTIVES

After completing Chapter 7, students will be able to:

- List the types of information that are exchanged between the travel agent and cruise reservationist when booking a cruise.

- Define the option date as it relates to the cruise reservation.

- Interpret all information printed on a typical cruise confirmation notice or invoice.

- Review the cruise cost procedures in terms of three distribution channels: the client, the travel agency, and the cruise line.

- List and describe the types of passenger documentation that are sent to the travel agency for the client after final payment has been made.

KEY TERMS

air/sea packages

baggage tags

cruise confirmation/invoice

cruise ticket

immigration questionnaire

miscellaneous charges order (MCO)

option date

port charges

Making the Cruise Reservation

Once the travel agent and his clients have decided on a specific ship, departure date, and cabin category, it is time to start the booking process. Unlike airline flights, most cruises are done by telephone; the airline computer reservation systems used by travel agencies have very limited capability at this time in terms of cruise information and booking capabilities. All cruise line reservation centers have toll-free numbers.

How to Prepare for the Call

In most cases, the initial booking call is made in front of the client. The cruise lines allow you to place a *temporary hold* on a cabin in a desired category for several days without payment. Therefore, a successful sales agent stresses the importance of contacting the cruise line *now*—not later—to make a booking; the cabin that the clients want today may not be available tomorrow!

The telephone call should be conducted in a smooth and professional manner; you should be fully prepared for the call. To expedite the booking transaction, you should always have the following information ready *before your call*:

- passenger name(s)
- total number in party
- ship and sailing date
- alternate ship and/or sailing date
- accommodation desired (type of cabin, category or cabin number)
- price range

If the cabin your clients want is free to sell, the cruise reservationist will place a temporary hold on the cabin. The reservationist then will confirm the following:

- cruise ship and sailing date
- length of the cruise
- cabin category and number that is on hold
- airfare supplements (if applicable)
- cruise cost
- port charges (tax amounts imposed by individual ports of call)
- option date for deposit

When a travel agent books a cruise, the cruise reservationist places a temporary hold on the cabin of choice. The cabin isn't actually confirmed or secured until the deposit is received by the cruise line. Usually, the deposit is required seven to ten days after the booking is made. Final payment is usually due 45–60 days before departure.

The following are some important questions and answers related to the option and payment process when booking cruises:

What is the cruise option? It is the final date when the deposit must be received by the cruise line in order to secure the cabin of choice. Usually, the option date is seven to ten days after the booking is made.

What happens if the deposit is not received by the option date? The cruise line has the right to cancel the booking immediately. Whatever cabin they were holding for your client is lost.

What should you do if you know that the deposit won't be received by the option date? The travel agent should immediately contact the reservations office to request an extension. The cruise line will usually extend the option by a few days. Remember: *if the option cannot be met, make sure you contact reservations on or before the option date in order to be granted an extension.*

Transmitting Payment: Agency Check or MCO

Deposits and final payments for cruise bookings are issued by sending the travel agency's check for the appropriate amount; personal checks from clients are not accepted by the cruise line. For credit card payment, most cruise lines will accept a *miscellaneous charges order* (*MCO*) as payment.

MCO forms are issued by the Airlines Reporting Corporation (ARC). The ARC also prints and distributes to travel agencies other airline-related forms, such as airline tickets and refund documents. The MCO is designed to record a deposit or final payment for a wide variety of air and land services such as airline tickets, hotel accommodations, land package tours, and cruises.

If the cruise line accepts MCOs for payment, the travel agent completes the MCO form, which indicates the following data: customer's name, reservation information (sailing date, cabin category, name of ship), and deposit or full payment amount. The client's credit card information is also recorded. A copy of the MCO is sent to the cruise line.

Figure 7.1 is a completed MCO for a deposit on an air/sea cruise on Norwegian Cruise Line. The MCO is being sent to transmit a deposit in the amount of $400.00 that is being charged to the customer's credit card.

NAME OF PASSENGER (NOT TRANSFERABLE)
HAYWARD/JOHN MR/MRS

MISCELLANEOUS CHARGES ORDER
AUDITOR'S COUPON

RATE OF EXCHANGE

8032:662:112

TOUR NO

EQUIVALENT AMOUNT PAID

PLACE OF ISSUE – AGENCY 87

TYPE OF SERVICE FOR WHICH ISSUED
DEPOSIT ON AIR/SEA CRUISE

01OCT
DATE OF ISSUE
VALID FOR ONE YEAR FROM DATE OF ISSUE

FARE/OTHER 400.00
U.S. TAX
OTHER TAX

MAGNOLIA TRAVEL
ATLANTA GA
00 12345 6

VALUE FOR EXCHANGE 1
AMOUNT IN LETTERS: FOUR HUNDRED DOLLARS & 00/100 CTS
CURRENCY
AMOUNT IN FIGURES: 400.00

TOTAL 400.00
COMM RATE 10
VOID IF MUTILATED OR ALTERED

TO: NORWEGIAN CRUISE LINE
AT: MIAMI FL
VALID FOR SPECIFIED SERVICES ONLY

ISSUED IN CONNECTION WITH

RESERVATION DATA
9DEC–16DEC SEAWARD, CAT. 10, CABIN #6046

FORM OF PAYMENT
AX 0000 7654 63621

REMARKS

IT IS UNLAWFUL TO PURCHASE OR RESELL THIS TICKET FROM/TO ANY ENTITY OTHER THAN THE ISSUING CARRIER OR ITS AUTHORIZED AGENTS

ENDORSEMENTS RESTRICTIONS (CARBON)

ISSUED BY
DELTA AIRLINES 006
SUBJECT TO TERMS AND CONDITIONS ON BACK OF PASSENGER'S COUPON

ISSUED IN EXCHANGE FOR
COMMISSION 10
TAB 0

CARRIER FORM SERIAL NUMBER
ORIGINAL ISSUE PLACE DATE AGENT'S NUMERIC CODE

CPN ⊙
AIRLINE CODE FORM SERIAL NUMBER CK
8032662112 2

Figure 7.1 **A completed miscellaneous charges order (MCO).**

The Cruise Confirmation/Invoice

The cruise line sends a cruise confirmation or invoice to the travel agency after the booking is made or after the deposit is received. The following information is usually indicated on the invoice:

- passenger name(s)
- dining requests
- deposit amount received/due date (if not already paid)
- reservation data/cabin assignment
- cost breakdown
- final payment due date

Figure 7.2 is a reproduction of a confirmation notice/invoice from Holland America Line. This was received after a $200.00-per-person deposit was received.

Checkpoint 7.1

Refer to Figure 7.2 and answer the following questions.

1. What are the passengers' names? ____________________
2. On which cruise ship are they confirmed? ____________________
3. What is their departure date? ____________________

```
HOLLAND AMERICA LINE
WESTTOURS INC.                            BOOKING
PO BOX C34013                             CONFIRMATION
SEATTLE, WASHINGTON 98124-1013            DATE OF INVOICE: 6/1/99
─────────────────────────────────────────────────────────────────
Full Name of Guests                       BOOKING CONFIRMATION:  582025-R
   Mr. Edward Summer
   Mrs. Harriet Summer
(PARTY OF 2 ADTS)


SAILING DATE: Nov 11, 1999                Optional cancellation
VESSEL: NIEUW AMSTERDAM                    Fee waiver and baggage
Accept
FROM: TAMPA FL                            Protection charges.
TO: TAMPA FL                              Check one:   Accept ☐  Decline ☐
NO. NIGHTS: 7        Cruise fares         $2,800.00
STATEROOM: 595       AIR SUPPLEMENT             0
CATEGORY: D          TOTAL CRUISE         $2,800.00
                     PORT CHARGE          $  250.00
LATE SEATING REQ     Sub Total            $3,050.00
TABLE FOR 8 REQ      Less commission      $  280.00 cr
                     Payment to date      $  400.00 cr
                     Amount due           $2,370.00     DUE OCT 11, 1999


ATT: BETTY AGENT # 617-555-1214   MAKE YOUR CHECK PAYABLE TO HOLLAND AMERICA LINE.
WORLDLY TRAVEL                     PO BOX C34013
1334 COMMONWEALTH AVE             SEATTLE WA 98124-1013
BOSTON MA    02215
```

Figure 7.2 Cruise confirmation/invoice.

4. What is the confirmation number for this booking? _____

5. What meal seating did these clients request—early or late? _____

6. What is the port of embarkation? _____

7. Where does this cruise terminate? _____

8. What cabin category is confirmed? _____

9. What is their cabin number? _____

10. Fill in the cost information:

    a. $_____ = Total cruise fare for two

    b. $_____ = Total port charges for two

c. $\underline{\hspace{2cm}}$ = Total cost (a + b)

d. $\underline{\hspace{2cm}}$ = Agency commission (10% of a)

e. $\underline{\hspace{2cm}}$ = Deposit sent

f. $\underline{\hspace{2cm}}$ = Balance payment due (c − d − e = f)

11. When is the final payment due? $\underline{\hspace{4cm}}$

12. Who made this reservation and at what travel agency? $\underline{\hspace{3cm}}$

FINAL PAYMENT AND DOCUMENTATION

Approximately 45–60 days before sailing, the cruise line requires final payment. The final payment is calculated this way:

> Total cost (cruise fare plus port charges and other fees)
> − Agency commission (standard is 10 percent of cruise fare)
> − Deposit sent in advance
> = Final payment

There are three channels of distribution when costing a cruise and sending payment: the client, the travel agency, and the cruise line. For example:

SS *Rotterdam*, Party of Two

Cruise fare = $1,500.00 per person
Port charges = $ 100.00 per person
Deposit   = $ 200.00 per person

Here is the breakdown of final payment for the client, the travel agency, and the cruise line.

The Client's Final Payment Is:	The Travel Agency Earns:	The Cruise Line Receives:
$3,000.00 cruise fare	$3000.00 cruise fare	$3,000.00 cruise fare
+ 200.00 port charges	× 0.10 commission	+ 200.00 port charges
− 400.00 deposit paid	= $ 300.00 commission	3,200.00 total cost
$2,800.00 balance due	earned	
		− 400.00 deposit paid
		− 300.00 agency commission
		$2,500.00 balance

Checkpoint 7.2 _____

The followng is a sample cruise cost chart for the cruise ship SS *Rotterdam*. For each exercise, complete all cost entries using this chart.

CATEGORY and CABIN DESCRIPTION			7-NIGHT CRUISE FARES			
			LOW	ECONOMY	VALUE	PEAK
			May 26	June 2, 9 Sep 1, 8	June 16 Aug 18, 25	June 23– Aug 11
☐ A Staterooms Deluxe	🛁 🚿		$2399	$2499	$2599	$2699
■ B Deluxe Outside Twin	🛁 🚿		1899	1999	2099	2199
☐ C Large Outside Twin	🛁 🚿		1799	1899	1999	2099
■ D Large Outside Twin	🛁 🚿		1749	1849	1949	2049
☐ E Outside Twin	🛁 🚿		1699	1799	1899	1999
■ F Outside Twin	🛁 🚿		1649	1749	1849	1949
■ G Outside Twin	🚿		1549	1649	1749	1849
■ H Economy Outside Upper/Lower	🚿		1299	1399	1499	1599
☐ I Large Inside Twin	🛁 🚿		1399	1499	1599	1699
☐ J Inside Twin	🚿		1299	1399	1499	1599
■ K Inside Twin	🚿		1249	1349	1449	1549
☐ L Inside Twin or Double	🚿		1199	1299	1399	1499
■ M Inside Twin or Double	🚿		1149	1249	1349	1449
■ N Inside Twin or Double	🚿		1049	1149	1249	1349
■ O Economy Inside Upper/Lower	🚿		999	1099	1199	1299
☐ P Outside Single	🚿		1799	1899	1999	2099
■ Q Inside Single	🚿		1599	1699	1799	1899
PORT CHARGES			36	36	36	36

Facilities**   🛁 Bath   🚿 Shower

Prices shown are per person based on double occupancy.
Third and fourth person sharing with two full fare passengers pay $699.00 per person.
Single fare, when not specified, is 150% of applicable cabin rate.
**Not all staterooms within each category will have the facilities shown.
Refer to deck plans for specific facilities in each stateroom.

Figure 7.3 **Sample cruise cost chart, SS *Rotterdam*.**

1. **Reservation data:** Departure May 26
   Cabin category: G, outside twin
   Clients: party of two adults

   Deposit required: $200.00 per person

   Client: $_____ total cost (including port charges)

                     $_____ deposit due in advance

                     $_____ final payment due

   Travel Agency: $_____ cruise fare (without port charges)

                     $_____ commission amount (10 percent of
                     cruise fare)

   Cruise Line: $_____ cruise fare (without port charges)

                     $_____ port charges

                     $_____ total cost

                     $_____ deposit (received in advance)

                     $_____ agency commission

                     $_____ balance due

2. **Reservation data:** Departure August 18
   Cabin category: D, large outside twin
   Clients: party of two adults

   Deposit required: $200.00 per person

   Client: $_____ total cost (including port charges)

                     $_____ deposit due in advance

                     $_____ final payment due

   Travel Agency: $_____ cruise fare (without port charges)

                     $_____ commission amount (10 percent of
                     cruise fare)

   Cruise Line: $_____ cruise fare (without port charges)

                     $_____ port charges

                     $_____ total cost

                     $_____ deposit (received in advance)

                     $_____ agency commission

                     $_____ balance due

3. Reservation data: Departure June 23
                              Cabin category: C, large outside twin
                              Clients: party of three adults sharing one cabin

Deposit required: $200.00 per person

Client	
$_____	total cost (including port charges)
$_____	deposit due in advance
$_____	final payment due

Travel Agency:	
$_____	cruise fare (without port charges)
$_____	commission amount (10 percent of cruise fare)

Cruise Line:	
$_____	cruise fare (without port charges)
$_____	port charges
$_____	total cost
$_____	deposit (received in advance)
$_____	agency commission
$_____	balance due

CRUISE DOCUMENTATION

After final payment is received by the cruise line, all travel documents are sent to the travel agency. Documents for a cruise are inserted in a cruise line document jacket and usually include the following materials:

Cruise Ticket

The cruise ticket looks different from a standard airline ticket. What it does have in common is the pertinent data regarding the passenger's cruise booking. Read through the sample ticket in Figure 7.4. What types of reservation data appear on it?

Baggage Tags

It is very important to advise your cruise clients to complete the baggage tags and attach them to each piece of luggage before they depart. On the day of embarkation, the clients surrender their luggage either at the airport upon arrival (if an air/sea package) or at dockside (if independent). Baggage is transported to the ship and cabin number indicated on the baggage tags. Each baggage tag must clearly identify the passenger's name, ship, sailing date, and cabin number. A sample baggage tag is shown in Figure 7.5.

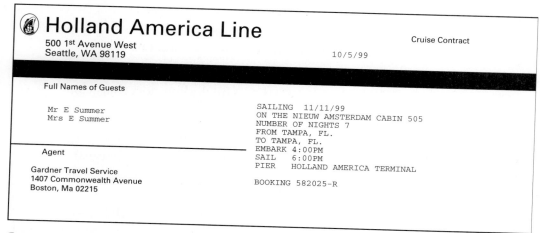

Holland America Line

500 1st Avenue West
Seattle, WA 98119

Cruise Contract

10/5/99

Full Names of Guests

Mr E Summer
Mrs E Summer

SAILING 11/11/99
ON THE NIEUW AMSTERDAM CABIN 505
NUMBER OF NIGHTS 7
FROM TAMPA, FL.
TO TAMPA, FL.
EMBARK 4:00PM
SAIL   6:00PM
PIER   HOLLAND AMERICA TERMINAL

Agent

Gardner Travel Service
1407 Commonwealth Avenue
Boston, Ma 02215

BOOKING 582025-R

Figure 7.4 **Sample cruise ticket.**

Immigration Questionnaire

Advise your clients to complete this important document before their departure. It is surrendered along with the cruise ticket before boarding the ship. This form establishes citizenship and allows the passenger to debark from the ship in the non-U.S. ports of call on the itinerary. A sample immigration questionnaire is shown in Figure 7.6.

Advise your clients of all required travel documents such as passports and proof of citizenship in plenty of time before departure. This information is explained in the cruise brochure under "Terms and Conditions."

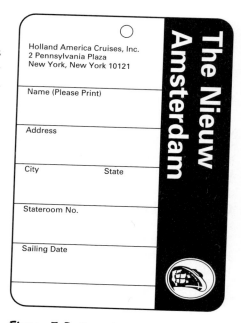

Holland America Cruises, Inc.
2 Pennsylvania Plaza
New York, New York 10121

Name (Please Print)

Address

City   State

Stateroom No.

Sailing Date

The Nieuw Amsterdam

Figure 7.5 **Sample baggage tag.**

General Information

Helpful information regarding the ship is also included in the client's documentation. Included would be any of the following:

- deck plans
- shore excursions

Figure 7.6 Sample immigration questionnaire.

- descriptions of ports of call
- descriptions of ship facilities and services

Airline Tickets

Many cruise clients purchase air/sea packages. The total cost of an air/sea package includes the cruise and round-trip air transportation and transfer service between the airport and ship. In many cases, the cruise line issues the airline ticket and mails it along with the other documents. The agent should always check with the cruise line to find out who issues the ticket.

For independent passengers (not taking an air/sea package), the travel agent books the flight and issues airline tickets under normal procedures.

CHAPTER REVIEW

1. Define the option date as it relates to cruise bookings.

_____

_____

2. What should you do if you know you cannot meet the option date?

_____

_____

_____

3. When you make the initial cruise booking, the cabin you request for your clients is on a temporary hold. What does that mean?

_____

_____

4. Are most cruise bookings completed through the travel agency's computer reservation system? _____

5. What additional features are included in an air/sea package?

_____

6. In addition to an agency check, what other forms of payment may be used when sending a deposit or final balance to the cruise line?

_____

7. Your clients are booked on the following cruise:

Seven days on the *Sovereign of the Seas*.
Departure: October 7
Party of two adults
Cruise cost: $1,650.00 per person
Port charge: $150.00 per person
Deposit required: $100 per person

What is the total amount of the cruise plus port charges for these passengers? $_____

The agency's commission is 10 percent. What is the total amount of agency commission? $_____

If you already sent the required deposit, what is the final payment amount due to the cruise line several weeks before departure?

$_____

Glossary

Aft   Toward or near the stern or back of the ship.

Air/sea package   Cruise package that includes the basic cruise plus round-trip airfare, transfers, and baggage handling.

Amidships or **midships**   In or toward the part of the ship midway between the bow and the stern.

Balconied cabin   An outside passenger accommodation that has a private balcony or verandah.

Beam   The width of the ship at its widest point.

Berth   (1) A bed in a ship's cabin. (2) The location at the pier where the ship docks.

Boat deck   The deck where the lifeboats are located.

Bow   The front part of the ship.

Bridge   The navigational and command center of the ship; closed to passengers except upon invitation.

Bulkhead   An upright partition or wall dividing the ship into cabins and compartments.

Center of gravity   The fulcrum or balancing point of the ship; located at the point where a vertical and horizontal line are drawn through the middle of the ship. This area offers the smoothest ride.

Companionway or **stair tower**   An interior stairway on a ship.

Course   The direction in which the ship is headed; usually expressed in compass degrees.

Cruise Lines International Association (CLIA)   A trade organization that consists of representative cruise lines and travel agency affiliates. Two main objectives are (1) to market and promote cruise travel to the traveling public, and (2) to offer educational and training support to its member travel agencies.

Debark or **disembark**   To get off or exit the ship.

Deck   Any floor on a ship, inside or out.

Deck plan   A blueprint or floor plan of a ship's design.

Demographics   The statistical study of populations in reference to such things as age, budget, marital status, special interests, and hobbies.

Dock   A berth, pier, or quay.

Embark   To get on board a ship.

Fathom   A measurement of distance (usually depth) in the water; equal to six feet.

Forward   Toward or near the bow or front of the ship.

Free port   A port or place free of customs duty and most customs regulations.

Funnel   A smokestack or "chimney" of the ship.

Galley   The ship's kitchen.

Gangway   The opening through the ship's side and the corresponding ramp by which passengers embark or disembark.

Gross Registered Ton (GRT)   A measurement of 100 cubic feet of enclosed revenue space within a ship.

Hold   Interior space below the main deck for storage or cargo where passengers are not allowed.

Hull   The part of the ship that rests in the water; the frame or body of the ship, exclusive of the superstructure.

Inside cabin   Accommodations without a window or porthole; located in the interior of a ship.

Knot   A unit of speed equal to one nautical mile per hour (6,080.2 feet), as compared to a land mile of 5,280 feet.

Ladder   Any stairway on the outside areas of the ship.

Leeward   Away from the wind.

Lifeboats   Boats carried by a ship that are for use in an emergency.

Main deck   The longest deck on the ship; separates the hull and the superstructure.

Manifest   A list or invoice of a ship's passengers, crew, and cargo.

Megaship   A large cruise vessel that measures more than 65,000 GRT with more than 2,000 passengers.

Midships   See *Amidships*.

Open seating   No set time of service or table assignments in the ship dining room for a particular meal; passengers are allowed to be served at any time.

Outside cabin   Accommodations on a ship with a window or porthole.

Per diem   Priced on a per-day basis.

Pitch   The front-to-back (bow-to-stern) motion of a ship.

Port   The left side of the ship when facing toward the front or bow.

Porthole   Round window or opening on the side of the ship.

Port-intensive   Describes an itinerary that offers more ports of call and fewer days at sea.

Post-tour   A hotel land package offered at the end of a cruise, includes accommodations, transfers, and sightseeing.

Pre-tour   A hotel land package before a cruise, includes accommodations, transfers, and sightseeing.

Pullman berth   A bed on board a ship that is pulled down from the wall when in use and recessed into the wall when not in use during the day.

Quay (pronounced *key*)   A berth, dock, or pier.

Registry   The country whose laws the ship and its owners are obliged to obey, in addition to complying with the laws of the countries where the ship calls and/or embarks passengers.

Repositioning   Moving a cruise ship from one area to another due to seasonal changes; for example, from Alaska at the end of the summer season to the Caribbean for fall and winter itineraries. Repositioning cruises are frequently offered as special cruise segments.

Roll   The side-to-side motion of the ship.

Seating times   Scheduled times when certain meals are served in the formal dining room of a ship. Usually there are two seatings: main (early) and second (late).

Space ratio   A way to measure how much space is occupied by one passenger if a full complement of passengers is sailing; equals GRT divided by standard passenger capacity.

Stabilizers   Fin-like, gyroscopically operated devices that extend from both sides of the ship below the waterline to provide a more stable motion. This device acts like a wing on an airplane.

Stack   A funnel from which the ship's combustion gases are freed to the atmosphere.

Standard passenger capacity   The total number of passengers on a ship if all cabins are occupied by two passengers.

Starboard   The right side of the ship facing forward.

Stem   The extreme forward point on the ship.

Stern   The back end of the ship.

Suite   The most expensive type of passenger accommodation; generally consists of a sitting area, one or two bedrooms, a kitchenette facility, and a verandah.

Superstructure   The part of the ship above the hull.

Table assignments   Assigned tables in the dining room for scheduled meals; they accommodate anywhere from two to ten people.

Tender   A smaller vessel, sometimes one of the ship's lifeboats, that is used to transport passengers between the ship and shore when the ship is at anchor.

Traditional cruise   The most popular and prevalent type of cruise, in which the ship is an all-inclusive resort that includes accommodations, transportation, dining, entertainment, recreation, and so on.

Upper and lower   Berth arrangements in a cabin that are similar to bunk beds.

Weather deck   Any deck open to the outside.

Weather side   The side of the ship that is exposed to the wind or to weather.

Windjammer   A tall-masted sailing ship that recreates sailing of earlier times; the "barefoot" variety allows passengers to actively participate in the sailing of the vessel.

Windward   Toward the wind.